Endorsements

This series of five studies is an excellent introduction to the interconnected challenges facing humanity in the 21st century - climate change, pandemics, the degradation of the biosphere, and the growing inequalities within and between countries. There is much to be learned from exploring ourselves and our contemporary societies - values, behaviours, systems, communities and responsibilities.

Will Steffen, Emeritus Professor, Australian National University and Councillor, Climate Council of Australia.

As it happens, I read these important ABM Studies on climate change the day after a new grandchild child was born. Like those reading this, as a matter of faith and love, I want to ensure everything I do brings well-being to her and all God's children. Please read together and apply the insights of these brilliant Studies."

Bishop Philip Huggins, President, NCCA.

"The writer of the last book in the Bible sat on an island in the Mediterranean in the dying days of an empire. He pictured two alternative cities, one which featured frivolous consumption and was about to collapse, and one made from diamonds with a tree of life and a river of life. The diamonds appear to be human work, crafted into a beautiful gem that can last generations. The city was made of diamonds of hope. Climate for Change is a diamond. Treasure it!"

Peter Newman AO, Professor of Sustainability, Curtin University, Co-ordinating Lead Author in IPCC, and a member of St Pauls Beaconsfield, Perth.

Through each of the studies there is a realistic perspective on current global disasters, substantiated by reliable research and professional writings, but this is always balanced by Christian faith in hope. What could be a blistering attack on our human selfishness, neglect and abuse, instead becomes encouragement and assistance for each person to contribute in some way, however small, to bring about change.

Consequently, as ABM has done in the past, there is an opportunity for people to participate in necessary study ultimately leading to greater opportunities to love God, love our neighbours and all of creation.

The Reverend Kaye Pitman OAM, St George's Anglican Parish Maleny,Queensland.

As a grandparent, I hope very many of our parishes commit to this study guide. We start by exploring our experiences living through the COVID-19 pandemic together but need to look into our children's and grandchildren's future and what we, the people in the pews, can do to change it for the better. We need to act now.

I hope small groups and parishes all over Australia will gather round this study guide - in person or online - however we can. It is so important. I hope too that we will invite the young, those whose future we are considering, to join us, bringing their passion and anxiety, so we can form a groundswell of opinion together. We have the institution, they have the energy. We could bring about 'a new earth'.

Kathy Kozlowski, Parishioner, St Paul's Cathedral, Melbourne.

Climate for Change *by Russell Rollason*
Produced September 2020
ISBN: 978-0-6483444-4-5

Free pdf version, or to order hard copies:
www.abmission.org

. . . .

Anglican Board Of Mission - Australia Ltd
ABN 18 097 944 717

General Enquiries:
Anglican Board of Mission - Australia
Locked Bag Q4005
Queen Victoria Building
NSW 1230 Australia

International: +61 2 9264 1021
Local Call: 1300 302663
Fax: +61 2 9261 3560
Email: info@abmission.org.au

Street Address:
Level 6, 51 Druitt St
Sydney NSW 2000
Australia

ANGLICAN BOARD OF MISSION
Working for Love, Hope & Justice

Contents

How to use this Climate for Change study guide

Step 1: A suitable time

The *Season of Creation* (1 September to 4 October) is an excellent opportunity to discuss these five studies but they can be used whenever it suits your group. One study a week over five weeks would enable time to seek more information on issues that come up at each session.

Step 2: Forming a group

The studies are intended for small group discussion (6-10 people is ideal). To plan the meetings and introduce the studies, it is suggested a facilitator be nominated for all or each of the studies. The facilitator will arrange the meeting time and place and invite the participants. S/he will introduce the study, and/or invite one or two others to facilitate the discussion. It is up to the group to decide how long they wish to discuss each study. To get the first discussion started, invite the members to read the first study prior to the meeting.

Step 3: Introductions

At the first meeting of the group, make sure everyone knows each other. There are at least three ways to introduce the discussion:

• begin with the prayers and meditation in the box in the study;

• show a video mentioned in that particular study (they can be downloaded onto a USB stick and shown via a laptop or a smart TV);

• read through the whole study/or sections aloud together, each person reading a paragraph or two.

Step 4: Recap of key learning and actions

It may be of value at the opening of studies 2- 5 that you invite members of the group to recall their key learning from the previous study and also share any action they have taken or are planning to take individually or with others in their family, the Parish or other groups in which they are involved.

Step 5: Questions

The questions at the end of each study are just starting points for discussion. Some may be more thought-provoking than others. Use as you wish. It is important that the facilitator encourages each member of the group to speak. There are no silly questions and there are no right answers! The goal of the studies is to gain a better understanding of the challenges that lie ahead and agreement that each of us can contribute to a fairer, more just and sustainable world for all.

Step 6: Taking a dive

Study 1 raises difficult questions about inequality and racism in society. If your group wishes to dive deeper into these issues, additional material for discussion is available for free download from ABM.

Step 7: Investigate

Each study also includes a range of links to other reports and other organisations active on the topics of the study. Perhaps one or two in the group would like to follow up on some of these links and bring back their findings to the next meeting. The challenges discussed are huge! They are about the future of life and the world as we know it, but it is surprising how much movement there is internationally. Around the world people are taking action and it is inspiring and exciting to discover what is happening. Take time to explore some of the websites listed in this study. I am sure you will be excited and motivated as you discover how people around the world and across the churches are seizing this *climate for change*.

Step 8: Join the mission

Join the mission to save the creation, to share the resources of the earth, to love our neighbour, to do justice and walk humbly with our God. Take the opportunity to:

1. Seek ways in your parish or organisation to take steps to address the challenges. You can use suggestions in the studies, including tools for assessment and exploring what parishes are doing.

2. Explore ways you can support ABM's partners who are living and working on the frontline of the climate emergency.

3. Connect:
   - with young people concerned about climate change,

   - with neighbours, friends and work mates to discuss the urgency to reduce carbon emissions,

   - with organisations in your local region working for a fairer, more sustainable future, and

   - with your parliamentarians who have the responsibility to take action on our behalf to create a better world.

Step 9: Let us know how you went

When you have completed the studies, we would love to hear how you went. Send us a brief email to info@abmission.org.au and add a photo too!

Introduction

Our world is in crisis. The COVID-19 virus is causing a health and economic crisis. But the pandemic is just a window into the climate crisis that threatens our very civilisation.

The climate crisis is a health, economic, social and environmental crisis, but it is also a spiritual crisis. Why do we care so little about our grandchildren and the world they will inherit, that we are not prepared to cut our carbon emissions today to avoid a climate catastrophe? We can make lifestyle changes that help restore hope for future generations and protect the environment on which all of life depends, but progress is too slow. We may have already left it too late to steer the Titanic away from the approaching iceberg, to paraphrase climate scientist Professor Will Steffen.[1]

Climate for Change aims to help small groups to discuss and reflect on the urgent changes we need and to recognise our dependence on the creation that sustains and gives life to all.

The studies start with the conviction that climate change is real and predominantly caused by human activity. The scientific evidence is conclusive and climate change is already destroying lives. References on the nature and impacts of climate change are included for those who may have questions. (See Annex 2)

For too long the climate change debate in Australia has suffered from a lack of political support for the decisions leaders need to make. These studies hope to contribute to building a groundswell of commitment that makes change inevitable and helps it stick! We believe it's time for a national discussion on how we can achieve net zero emissions, to limit the global temperature rise to no more than 1.5°C above pre-industrial levels.

Central to the studies is the Christian conviction that all are created in God's image and all share the world's resources. Equity is a key theme. There can be no peace without justice.

Climate for Change seeks to strengthen hope through a determination to work with others to create a future for all. Our hope lies in the knowledge that God has not abandoned creation but rather has called us all to help restore and respect it.

The studies are a contribution to the global ecumenical **Season of Creation**.[2] Each year from September 1 to October 4, the

---

1 Steffen, Will. 'Collapse of Civilisation is the most likely outcome'. Resilience online 8 June 2020 https://www.resilience.org/stories/2020-06-08/collapse-of-civilisation-is-the-most-likely-outcome-top-climate-scientists/

2 https://seasonofcreation.org/about/

Christian family can unite for this worldwide celebration of prayer and action to protect our common home. A call to create a future for all echoes the **Sustainable Development Goals** (SDGs) adopted in 2015 by 193 countries. The SDGs provide a roadmap to ending global poverty, building a life of dignity for all and leaving no one behind.

For the sake of future generations, we must seize this opportunity to take action. Act not out of fear, but build on the hope we all share for a fairer, more just and peaceful world.

We share a faith grounded in hope, but hope requires action. Action out of hope will inspire others. That is the challenge of these studies. A national dialogue is urgent to create the groundswell for our leaders to take the decisions necessary to achieve zero carbon emissions before 2050. I hope these studies can add momentum to the groundswell that is already gathering speed, so all may look forward to a future of justice, peace and respect for the environment we depend on.

Acknowledgements

Special thanks to ABM for publishing these studies and to the team that ABM assembled to assist with valuable advice and guidance. The patient and committed team members are Brad Chapman (Reconciliation Missioner), the Rev'd Jazz Dow (Missioner), Brother Christopher John (Minister General, Society of St Francis), Dr Terry Russell (Effectiveness and Emergency Missioner), and Greg Thompson (ABM Board)

Thanks to Bruce Best (a former journalist on The Age, who taught me to write in the mid-1970s) for editing the final draft. Thanks to Canon Stephen Daughtry (Education Missioner) for assisting with the production and to Annette Zanker for her inspired design.

I greatly valued the comments and suggestions from a range of readers from around Australia. Thank you for taking the time to read and comment on the studies.

We all are most grateful for the generous grant from the Oikoumene Foundation and the personal donation from Professor Peter Newman. Their support has enabled the publication of these studies. The Oikoumene Foundation supports activities that contribute to a just, participatory and sustainable society.

May you be inspired to join with others in protecting and sustaining God's creation for all.

Russell Rollason, Newcastle, July 2020

About the author

Russell grew up in the Anglican Church in Brisbane and has served on synods in Sydney and Canberra as well as on the vestry for a Melbourne parish. He now lives in Newcastle, and his wife Tracey is Rector of the Anglican Parish of Glenrock. From 1998 to 2004, he was Executive Officer of Anglicare Australia based in Melbourne.

A science honours graduate from the University of Queensland (Geology and Mineralogy), Russell also holds a Masters in General Studies from the UNSW. After working as a geologist for three years, Russell felt called to act on international poverty. Thirty plus years later, his career in international aid and development has included working for a decade with the then Australian Council of Churches (now NCCA), 12 years as Executive Director of the Australian Council for Overseas Aid (now ACFID), 3 years as an international consultant and finally 14 years with AusAID, subsequently absorbed into the Department of Foreign Affairs and Trade (DFAT).

In 1998, he was appointed a Member of the Order of Australia, for services to international development and humanitarian aid through the Australian Council for Overseas Aid and promotion of social justice in Australia.

Russell's DFAT experience introduced him to global water issues. He was posted for 3 years as First Secretary in the Australian High Commission to India, responsible for expanding Australia's technical cooperation program with India in water resource management. After retiring from DFAT in 2019, Russell took up a part-time position as International Development Adviser with eWater, the organisation set up by the Federal and State governments to manage Australia's water modelling tools.

Russell's interest in climate change was sparked when visiting poor communities in Asia and Africa and seeing how drought and floods destroyed lives and livelihoods. It was also clear that climate change meant water change.

Water is critical to life - integral to all social, economic and environmental activities. Water underpins food production, electricity generation, livelihoods, life in cities and human health. But climate change is creating havoc with rainfall patterns, frequency and intensity. So much so that (fresh)water is becoming scarce around the world. The UN Secretary General has noted that *40% of the world's people are affected by water scarcity and by 2050, at least one in four people will live in a country where the lack of fresh water will be chronic or recurrent.*

The Season of Creation is an annual ecumenical observation from September 1 to St Francis of Assisi Day on October 4. It is appropriate that we celebrate the life of St Francis, the patron saint for animals and the environment. Here is a brief profile of St Francis, written by Br Christopher John SSF.

Francis of Assisi

Francis lived about 800 years ago in central Italy. It was a world and time very different from our own. Yet some of his ideas are very timely for us. He had an intuitive grasp of the relationship between all the parts of creation, and their creator. Everything in creation is part of an intricate web created by God. Each part speaks of God's presence and purpose.

Yet with this gift comes the responsibility to live in right relationship with each element. Francis called them sister and brother. This wasn't just weak sentimentality. He knew that he owed his life to earth and water and wind and sun and moon and stars—even fire.

He wrote a Canticle in Praise of the Creatures. By addressing them as brother or sister, he brings them into the closeness and intimacy of human relationship. He gives them a voice. They too offer to God their praises as we give God our praises for God's goodness. God has given us such a beautiful world for our home.

In the time of Francis the damage which humankind could inflict on creation was limited. But in our day the potential for destruction is so much greater. We are given an awesome responsibility. How do we use our God-given gifts of intelligence and creative skill to care for this planet Earth, our home? The voice of Francis from 800 years ago still calls out to us. How do we love those sisters and brothers God has given us in all the many and various parts of creation? What world do we give to the generations who come after us?

From Francis of Assisi and Scripture

"Let us desire nothing else, let us want nothing else, let nothing else please us and cause us delight except our Creator, Redeemer and Saviour, the only true God, who is the fulness of good."
Francis of Assisi – Earlier Rule 9.

"If you choose, you can keep the commandments, and to act faithfully is a matter of your own choice. He has placed before you fire and water; stretch out your hand for whichever you choose. Before each person are life and death, and whichever one chooses will be given. For great is the wisdom of the Lord; he is mighty in power and sees everything; his eyes are on those who fear him, and he knows every human action."
Ecclesiasticus 15:15-19 NRSV

Reflection and Prayer

We are living in a time which seems full of challenges. These can knock us down, sap our energy and life, and leave us feeling powerless. Yet God calls us to be in this place, to stand with others in their pain, to be bearers of hope and life. It is in such times perhaps we can recognise that we are standing on holy ground; that we are given the opportunity to turn and seek life, rather than being paralysed with fear.

Silence

Blessed are you, God of the moment of decision and turning. You place us in this holy place with all who have gone before us in struggle and uncertainty. Help us to choose life, to know that you are with us even when we cannot see you, and to see how this moment calls us to turn and embrace a new future as we stand with Jesus Christ our Saviour and Guide.

Amen.

1

The Coronavirus Pandemic: a 'dress rehearsal' for climate change

STUDY 1: KEY POINTS

- COVID-19 pandemic has provided a window on future climate threats.

- The poor and marginalised in our society have suffered most.

- We must learn the lessons from the pandemic.

- COVID-19 has also created an opportunity for 'a great reset'.

- A renewable path to the future as $billions are invested in economic recovery.

"Historically, pandemics have forced humans to break with the past and imagine the world anew. This one is no different. It is a portal, a gateway between one world and the next".
Arundhati Roy

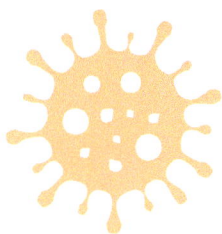

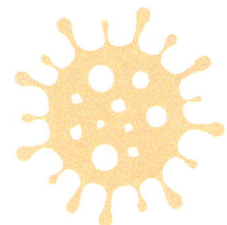

COVID-19 has disrupted our lives and caused widespread misery and suffering. It has laid bare the disparities of our world today: disparities in income and wealth, and access to healthcare, along with disparate outcomes based on age, race or gender. Climate change will have similar impacts, but it is going to be with us permanently.

However, the pandemic has also presented the world with a unique opportunity to take stock and, with courage, set a new course for a better, fairer world.

The poor and marginalised hit hardest

COVID-19 has caused immense harm to those living in poorer areas. Whether in rich countries or poor ones, people in poorer neighbourhoods often live in small homes they share with many generations of the family. Or they live in buildings with shared kitchens, toilets, water access, or with narrow corridors or lanes. They are more likely to have jobs that cannot be done from home. They do the essential work for urban life: public transport, healthcare, refuse collection, deliveries, or food service and supply. Those on the lowest incomes have found it hard or impossible to isolate at home. **Poorer neighbourhoods**[3] are more likely to have higher rates of pre-existing health problems, such as heart or lung disease. These can exacerbate the impact of the virus.

Many have observed that the virus affects princes and prime ministers alike. But that is where the equality ends. Social distancing is practically impossible if you live in a crowded slum in Mumbai or in a migrant worker hostel in Singapore. Hand-washing is impossible if you have no running water. Governments may tell people not to go out to work, but if that means their families will not eat, they will go out anyway. If prevented, they may riot.[4]

The coronavirus is causing havoc in rich countries, but it is devastating some poorer countries.

The UN has warned that the coronavirus crisis could push more than a quarter of a billion people to the brink of starvation unless swift action is taken to provide food and humanitarian relief to the most at-risk regions.

About 265 million people around the world are forecast to be facing acute food insecurity by the end of this year. That's double the 130 million estimated to have suffered severe food shortages last year. The **Global Report on Food Crises**[5], by the UN Food and Agriculture Organisation, the World Food Programme and 14 other organisations, published in April 2020, warns that global hunger could become the next big impact of the pandemic.

Photo credit: Francesca Del Soldata Aragone

3 https://www.washingtonpost.com/nation/2020/04/07/coronavirus-is-in-fecting-killing-black-americans-an-alarmingly-high-rate-post-analy-sis-shows/?arc404=true

4 McFarlane, Colin. 'The urban poor have been hit hard by coronavirus'. Urban Geography, Durham University. The Conversation 3 June 2020

5 https://www.wfp.org/publications/2020-global-report-food-crises

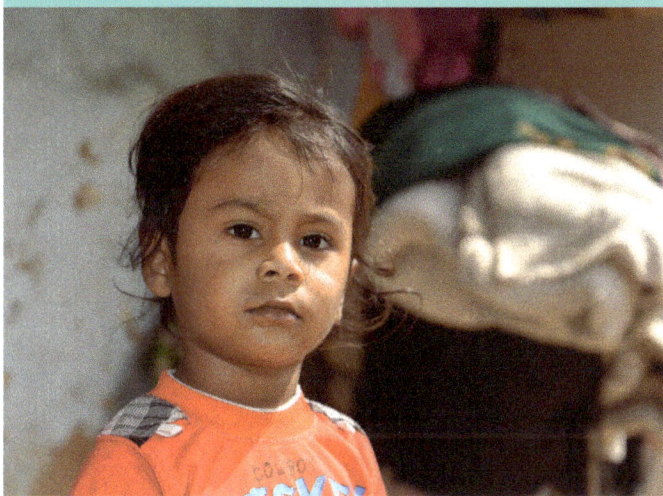

Photo credit: Francesca Del Soldata Aragone

A dress rehearsal for climate change?

Chair of the Commission for the Human Future and former Liberal Party leader Professor John Hewson said on releasing **"Surviving and Thriving in the 21st Century"**:[6]

"The coronavirus pandemic should be seen as a dress rehearsal for what awaits us if we continue to ignore the laws of science, the physical world and the demands of several catastrophic threats such as climate change."

The COVID-19 crisis and the climate / biodiversity crises are deeply connected, according to infectious disease and environmental health experts around the world. These experts work on 'planetary health'. This connects human health, civilisation and the natural systems on which they depend. In a ground-breaking 2015 report by the Rockefeller Foundation and *The Lancet* medical journal, the scientists observed:

"Health effects from changes to the environment including climatic change, ocean acidification, land degradation, water scarcity, overexploitation of fisheries, and biodiversity loss pose serious challenges to the global health gains of the past several decades and are likely to become increasingly dominant during the second half of this century and beyond."[7]

The COVID-19 pandemic is a crisis of our own making. Our 'war' on nature has led to nature's 'war' on us. Pioneering 20th century conservationist Rachel Carson recognized this in the 1950s in her best-selling book *Silent Spring*. A war on nature is ultimately a war against ourselves.

Pope Francis made a similar point in his 2015 Encyclical, *Care for our Common Home,* when he said, "If we destroy Creation, Creation will destroy us".

On World Environment Day, United Nations Secretary General Antonio Guterres said, "Protecting the planet and ecosystems will be crucial to preventing further pandemics . To care for humanity, we must care for nature."

6 https://humanfuture.net/sites/default/files/CHF_Roundtable_Report_March_2020.pdf

7 Safeguarding human health in the Anthropocene epoch: report of The Rockefeller Foundation–Lancet Commission on planetary health. 15 July 2015 https://www.thelancet.com/commissions/planetary-health

Everything is connected

The world has an insatiable appetite for resources and an ever-expanding human population. Where has this led? "We invade tropical forests and other wild landscapes, which harbour so many species of animals and plants—and within those creatures, so many unknown viruses," David Quammen, author of *Spillover: Animal Infections and the Next Pandemic*[8], wrote in the *New York Times*.

"We cut the trees; we kill the animals or cage them and send them to markets. We disrupt ecosystems, and we shake viruses loose from their natural hosts. When that happens, they need a new host. Often, we are it."

The US organisation, Eco-Health Alliance, specialises in wildlife-borne diseases. It has estimated that there may be 1.7 million mystery coronaviruses in wildlife that have the potential to transfer to humans and cause more pandemics.[9] Sixty percent of the infectious diseases that emerged from 1990 to 2004 came from animals.

This pandemic provides unprecedented and powerful proof that nature and people share the same fate and are more closely linked than most of us realised.[10]

What has become clear over past months, through the smoke of the bushfire crisis, is that we are intimately connected to nature, to the ecosystem. We are all in this together.

Photo credit: Russell Rollason

8 Quammen, David. Spillover: Animal Infections and the next Pandemic. WW Norton and Coy. New York 2013

9 https://www.ecohealthalliance.org/

10 High Ambition Coalition for Nature and People. https://www.campaignfornature.org/home

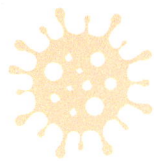

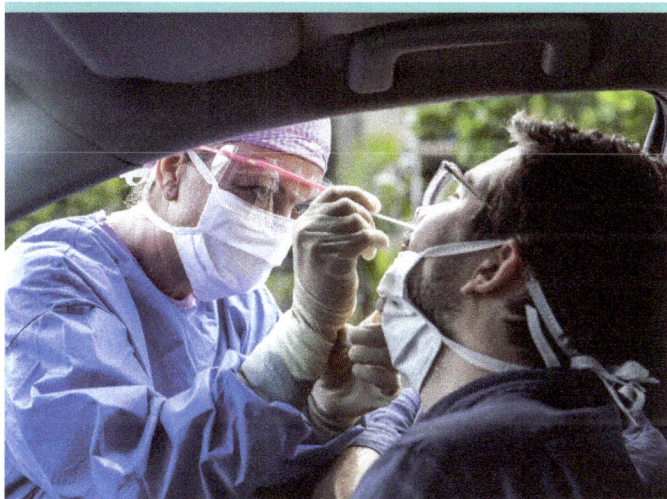

Photo credit: Adobe Stock

Lessons for our response to climate change

We still have much to learn about and from this pandemic, but some early lessons have been chalked up:

Science and facts are back at centre stage. Few coronavirus deniers have found a voice. The importance of science informing decisions about climate change is just as critical as it has been in COVID-19.[11]

Government is also back at centre stage. The market has proven incapable of responding to the pandemic. It requires Government leadership and resources to tackle the pandemic.

Central to saving lives in the pandemic has been **engaging society in behavioural change**, especially social / physical distancing and isolation. When the goal is clear and the reasons for action have been adequately explained, most people are willing to change their behaviour for the greater common good. This behavioural change lesson is critical to our responses to the climate challenge.

'Go early and go hard' has become a catchcry for responding to COVID-19. By implementing strong social restrictions immediately after the first COVID-19 case, several countries have been able to significantly reduce their infection rates and total infections. Procrastination has been costly. 'Go early and go hard' must also become the catchcry for climate change action. We are too late to go early, but if we do not make deep cuts to emissions beginning this year, our failure may well cost the earth.

11 Ajay Gambhir Grantham Institute blog
   http://www.lse.ac.uk/GranthamInstitute/

Image coutesy of Brenna Quinlan and ARRCC

A portal to the next world: Shaping the post-COVID future

The COVID-19 crisis, and the political, economic and social disruptions it has caused, is fundamentally changing the traditional context for decision-making, according to the World Economic Forum (WEF). "The inconsistencies, inadequacies and contradictions of multiple systems – from health and financial to energy and education – are more exposed than ever amidst a global context of concern for lives, livelihoods and the planet. Leaders find themselves at a historic crossroads, managing short-term pressures against medium- and long-term uncertainties," says the WEF.[12]

Seeing a unique window of opportunity to shape the post-COVID recovery, WEF Executive Chairman Professor Klaus Schwab, HRH The Prince of Wales and the Managing Director of the International Monetary Fund, Dr Kristalina Georgieva, launched a Great Reset initiative. It aims to build a new social contract that honours the dignity of every human being. The Great Reset[13] -rebuilding the global economy in a fairer, greener way as we come out of the coronavirus pandemic – will also require societies to battle and beat racism, according to Professor Schwab. For IMF chief Georgieva, it will mean a "greener, smarter, fairer world".

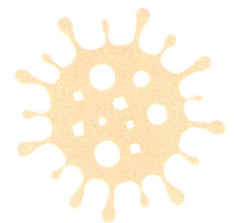

12 The Great Reset. World Economic Forum.
https://www.weforum.org/great-reset/

13 https://www.weforum.org/great-reset/

On Earth Day 2020, the **Interfaith group** active at UN Climate Change conferences recognised that "plans for a just recovery from COVID-19 must take into account the necessary measures to tackle climate change with a managed, planned and fair approach".

"The choices we now make will shape our society for years and it is crucial that efforts to rebuild economies put people's health before profit. ... We must not return to relaunching fossil fuel subsidies and unhealthy consumption patterns," said the Interfaith group.

In early April 2020, seventeen European climate and environment ministers urged their nations to "prepare ourselves to rebuild our economy and to introduce the necessary recovery plans to bring renewed, sustainable progress and prosperity back to Europe and its citizens".

"While doing so, we must not lose sight of the persisting climate and ecological crisis. Building momentum to fight this battle has to stay high on the political agenda," said the Ministers.

Achim Steiner, head of the **UN Development Programme** (UNDP), observed "the post-coronavirus stimulus packages must shift the economy away from its 'irrational' oil dependence to a greener future".

Steiner told *Climate Home News* in a video interview from New York, "You have an opportunity to either invest in returning to yesterday's economy or to invest into tomorrow's economy."

Watch the video:

At the launch of the WEF Great Reset, British economist Lord Nick Stern said: "This is a story of hope, vision, practicability and delivery. We can do all these things."

And it seems like the international community may be ready to work for a better future.

A recent survey across six nations revealed that the coronavirus pandemic is unleashing shifts in attitudes that would usually take years to trickle down. "COVID-19 has also prompted more people to want to work for organisations committed to social improvement," Dutch research agency Glocalities told the Thomson Reuters Foundation. "There's a lot of opportunity now for change because in times of crisis, things become more fluid, and changes can happen much faster."

COVID-19 has created a climate for change.

Discussion

- What have you learned from the pandemic? How do you think the pandemic has changed Australia / the world?

- Do you agree that the pandemic has created a unique opportunity to change the way the world is organised?

- Do we as Christians bring any special contribution to discussions about how the world is organised? If so, what is the perspective that people of faith can offer?

- Do you think it wise to link the global challenges of climate change, inequality, racism and environmental protection in trying to influence how Governments spend the billion dollar pandemic stimulus/ recovery packages?

- What do you hope will be the hallmarks of a post-COVID world? What do you think our faith requires as hallmarks of society?

Action

1. Search online for plans and programs that have been developed outlining how the stimulus package for COVID-19 can help create a low carbon future and help avoid dangerous climate change.

2. View the video presentation of the Great Reset (there is a short introductory one as well as a one hour video from the launch with a range of short presentations) and discuss the issues raised. Alternatively, view *Primed for Action* (1min 40 sec) from the Climate Council and discuss.

3. Arrange a meeting with your Federal MP to discuss if he/she will support the application of the stimulus package to promote jobs in renewable energy and other low carbon initiatives.

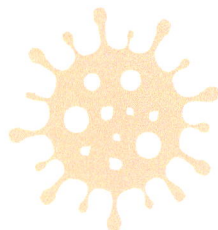

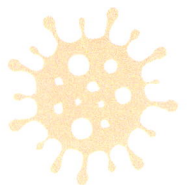

Resources

The Rockefeller Foundation–*Lancet* Commission on planetary health, *Safeguarding human health in the Anthropocene epoch.* 15 July 2015 https://www.thelancet.com/commissions/planetary-health

Glasser, Robert: *Preparing for the era of disasters.* Australian Strategic Policy Institute, 2019 https://www.aspi.org.au/report/preparing-era-disasters

2020 The Global Report on Food Crises. World Food Program, Rome, 2020. https://www.wfp.org/publications/2020-global-report-food-crises

Interfaith Summit on Climate Change. https://interfaithclimate.org/

Eddo-Lodge, Rene: "Why I am no longer talking to White People about Race". London: Bloomsbury, 2017.

Lindsay, Ben:. "We need to talk about Race". London: SPCK, 2019

Videos

The Great Reset: https://www.weforum.org/great-reset/

Primed for Action: Setting Australia up as a global powerhouse. The Climate Council. https://www.climatecouncil.org.au/resource/videos/

Tracking progress on the Sustainable Development Goals https://experience.arcgis.com/experience/8946bbc4090749c2aa1b6c1c80999bc6

Bible Study

Facing the Red Sea: Overcoming Fear by Using Your Gifts, Bible study by Joy Eva Bohol, 11 June 2020 https://www.oikoumene.org/en/resources/documents/wcc-programmes/facing-the-red-sea-overcoming-fear-by-using-your-gifts-bible-study-by-joy-eva-bohol/

From Francis of Assisi and Scripture

"I have done what is mine; may Christ teach you yours."
Francis of Assisi – as quoted in Bonaventure's Major Legend 14:3

"Besides this, you know what time it is, how it is now the moment for you to wake from sleep. For salvation is nearer to us now than when we became believers; the night is far gone, the day is near. Let us then lay aside the works of darkness and put on the armour of light; let us live honourably as in the day, … put on the Lord Jesus Christ, and make no provision for the flesh, to gratify its desires."
Romans 13: 11-14 NRSV

Reflection and Prayer

Our faith calls us to much more than just believing in God, or praying or worshiping. God calls us to work in this world, to be agents of the Divine. In the midst of many choices, we need to discern God's will, trusting that God gives us all that we need for this task. And we need to act, for to do nothing is to refuse God's invitation of cooperation.

Silence

Blessed are you, God of action. You have placed us in this world you love to work with you. We are the people called to put on Christ, to be Christ's presence, to be light where there is darkness. You have given us knowledge and skill, vision and creativity, the will and passion to work for a world in which your presence shines through all creation and all can flourish. May we live and act to the glory of Jesus Christ, in whose name we pray.

Amen.

2

Action on Climate Change is critical and urgent

STUDY 2: KEY POINTS

- Action to avert a climate catastrophe is urgent.

- We need to halve Australia's emissions in the next ten years, beginning now.

- The cost of the change must be shared, not just left to those whose jobs disappear.

Greta Thunberg, the Swedish school girl who started the global student strikes for climate action, spoke at the World Economic Summit in Davos, Switzerland, in January, 2019. She told delegates,

"I want you to act as you would in a crisis. I want you to act as if your house is on fire. Because it is".

The issues

Climate change is one of the 21st century's most pervasive global threats to human development, peace and security. As we have seen in Australia, climate change impacts primarily through the water cycle, leading to harsh long-term droughts and intense storms and flash flooding. The world's population is increasing, leading to rising demand for food, energy and water. Supplying this extra food, energy and water is being exacerbated by climate change, straining resources and potentially contributing to conflict and displacement.

The recent World Economic Forum Global Risks Report states: "Failure of climate change mitigation and adaption" is the number one risk by impact and number two by likelihood over the next 10 years.

▶ **Watch the video** (3.5 mins): Greta Thunberg and George Monbiot: https://youtu.be/-QOxUXo2zEY

A clear target

In Paris in 2015, 195 countries under the United Nations Framework Convention on Climate Change adopted the Paris Agreement. This set out a plan to avoid dangerous climate change by limiting global warming to below 2°C and pursuing efforts to limit it to 1.5°C above pre-industrial levels by 2050.

The United Nations and the international community are kept informed about climate change by the Intergovernmental Panel on Climate Change (IPCC). The panel of leading scientists from around the world was set up in 1988 to provide regular scientific assessments on the progress of climate change.

In October 2018, the IPCC provided an authoritative new report that set the world a clear target: we must reduce emissions of greenhouse gases to net zero by the middle of this century to have a reasonable chance of limiting global warming to 1.5°C.[14]

The safe limit for temperature increase is recognised as 1.5°C. But if we continue on a "business as usual" basis, global temperature could rise by more than 4°C. This level of temperature increase would be catastrophic (IPCC, 2014). It would mean a world of unprecedented heatwaves, severe drought, bushfires, flooding, inundation of many cities and other land, and major storms.

Christiana Figueres, former head of the UN Framework Convention on Climate Change (UNFCCC), summed up the ground-breaking IPCC October 2018 in three points:

"If global temperatures rise above the agreed limit of 1.5°C to 2°C, the world will see

- twice as many biodiversity species lost,

- twice as much infrastructure and economic value destroyed, and

- three times as many people will be exposed to water scarcity, food insecurity, and temperatures at home that make home uninhabitable."

These events have serious impacts on all human systems and ecosystems, creating many climate refugees, increased mortality, and species' extinctions. We could expect forced migration, conflict and political chaos.

14 Global Warming of 1.5 °C – IPCC https://report.ipcc.ch/sr15/pdf/
    sr15_spm_final.pdf

Photo credit: Don Brice, Vanuatu

As Christians, we cannot turn away. We who pray 'give us today our daily bread' cannot impose our failure to share with justice the resources of the earth on future generations. That is why we have the moral responsibility to do all we can to keep climate change to 1.5°C and not open the door to 2°C.

But global temperatures continue to rise. All of the world's 10 warmest years on record have occurred since 1998.[15]

To keep the world's temperature increase to less than 1.5°C by the middle of the century (ie 2050) requires urgent action now to reduce carbon emissions (or greenhouse gases).

As Christiana Figueres states in her recent book, *The Future We Choose:*[16]

"We are in the critical decade. It is no exaggeration to say that what we do regarding emissions reductions between now and 2030 will determine the quality of human life on this planet for hundreds of years to come, if not more."

Climate change threatens our Island neighbours

For Pacific Islanders, "climate change remains the single greatest threat to the livelihoods, security and wellbeing of the peoples of the Pacific". This statement is at the heart of the Boe Declaration[17] signed at the 2018 Pacific Islands Forum by regional leaders (and Australia's Foreign Minister). Pacific Island countries are disproportionately affected by climate change even though they only account for approximately 0.4 percent of global greenhouse gas emissions. Torres Strait Islanders are as affected by climate change as their Pacific neighbours.

Pacific Island countries face the highest disaster risk, in per capita terms in the world. Most of them are located along the cyclone belt, and are either on or near the boundary between the Australian and Pacific tectonic plates. This exposes them to catastrophic events such as earthquakes and cyclones. They are vulnerable to tsunamis and storm surges generated offshore. They are also vulnerable to sea level rise caused by warming oceans and melting polar icecaps.

15 Climate Council 2015: Growing Risks, Critical Choices. https://www.climatecouncil.org.au/resources/climate-change-2015-growing-risks-critical-choices/

16 Christina Figueres. The Future We Choose: Surviving the Climate Crisis. Manilla Press, 2020.

17 Boe Declaration on Regional Security https://www.forumsec.org/2018/09/05/boe-declaration-on-regional-security/

Reweaving the ecological mat

The Anglican Board of Mission is committed to give high priority in its international activities to supporting the peoples of the South Pacific. ABM encourages a hospitable and human response to those who lose their land and livelihood to climate change and have no option but to seek refuge elsewhere.

Telling the **stories**[18] of climate change impacts and the efforts of local communities to adapt in the Pacific, Asia and Africa is an important role for ABM.

The Pacific Conference of Churches (PCC) has launched a programme, **Reweaving the Ecological Mat**[19], which ABM is actively supporting. With partners from civil society organizations and academic institutions like the University of the South Pacific, the PCC is building the foundations of an Ecological Framework for Development. This will guide its engagements with its members and offer to governments some alternatives on development.

What to do?

To achieve the target to keep the global temperature increase to less than 1.5C of the pre-industrial level, we will need to cut emissions and remove carbon dioxide and other greenhouse gases from the atmosphere to reduce and reverse emissions.

The main sectors for emissions reductions and the kind of actions needed include:

1. **Energy** — Generating electricity using fossil fuels (especially coal and gas) is a major source of carbon emissions today. To achieve net zero emissions by 2050, the world will need to make a rapid conversion to renewable energy. Good progress has been made. In Australia, there will need to be more investment in renewable energy, especially onshore wind turbines and utility-scale solar. There is also scope for capturing and storing carbon dioxide emissions from coal-fired power stations and the like through sequestration, bio-char, mineral carbonisation and other techniques.

2. **Food** – The production and distribution of food requires significant energy. Action is needed to reduce food waste (each year more than five million tonnes of food ends up in landfill in Australia), reform agriculture practices, and increase land

---

18 https://www.abmission.org/pages/solomon-islands-three-projects-2020.html

19 https://ptc.ac.fj/?page_id=2016

rehabilitation. To reduce carbon emissions from food production, we need to eat less meat and dairy (to reduce greenhouse gas emissions, deforestation, water shortages and ocean pollution)[20], rehabilitate degraded areas, protect soil carbon, regenerate forests, change agricultural practices, and restore degraded ecosystems.

3. **Industry** — The effort needed to reduce emission in industry includes significantly increasing energy efficiency, switching to alternative cements, recycling water and energy, and introducing bioplastics.

4. **Buildings** — Improving the efficient use of energy in houses, churches, offices and other buildings will reduce energy demand. Improved insulation and solar heating are two key steps.

5. **Transport** — COVID-19 has provided a glimpse of a world free of fossil fuel-based air travel and cars. Pollution disappeared and, in some places, like Delhi, the snow-capped Himalayas could be seen for the first time in a generation. Cities survived, people walked or cycled and information technology allowed people to meet and work virtually. We can reshape our transport future through electric vehicles, clean shipping, and electric rail all powered by renewable energy.

Check out what your state or city is doing about progress in one or more of these sectors. Do they have a plan? Discuss it at your next meeting. Can you help its implementation?

This is the transformational decade

Research shows that the years before 2030 offer a window for action that will not stay open.

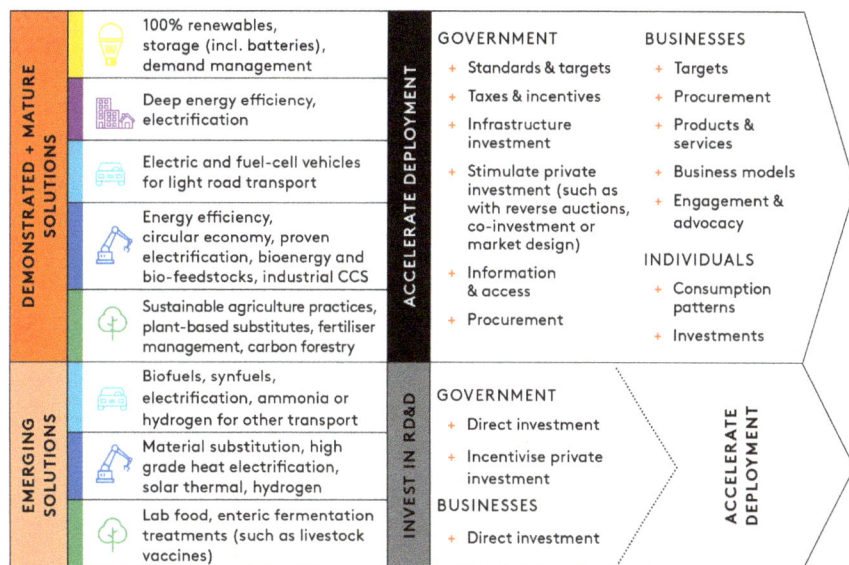

DEMONSTRATED + MATURE SOLUTIONS		ACCELERATE DEPLOYMENT	GOVERNMENT	BUSINESSES
	100% renewables, storage (incl. batteries), demand management		+ Standards & targets	+ Targets
	Deep energy efficiency, electrification		+ Taxes & incentives	+ Procurement
	Electric and fuel-cell vehicles for light road transport		+ Infrastructure investment	+ Products & services
	Energy efficiency, circular economy, proven electrification, bioenergy and bio-feedstocks, industrial CCS		+ Stimulate private investment (such as with reverse auctions, co-investment or market design)	+ Business models + Engagement & advocacy
	Sustainable agriculture practices, plant-based substitutes, fertiliser management, carbon forestry		+ Information & access	INDIVIDUALS + Consumption patterns
			+ Procurement	+ Investments

EMERGING SOLUTIONS		INVEST IN RD&D		ACCELERATE DEPLOYMENT
	Biofuels, synfuels, electrification, ammonia or hydrogen for other transport		GOVERNMENT + Direct investment	
	Material substitution, high grade heat electrification, solar thermal, hydrogen		+ Incentivise private investment	
	Lab food, enteric fermentation treatments (such as livestock vaccines)		BUSINESSES + Direct investment	

Source: ClimateWorks Australia, Decarbonisation Futures

20 Springmann, Marco. et al "Options for keeping the food systems within environmental limits. 2018 Nature.

But what can *we* do?

We all share the longing to move to a kinder more sustainable lifestyle through conserving the earth's resources and protecting the ecosystem on which we all depend.

There is much that we and our community can do to reduce our carbon footprint. There are also many great guides, available from churches, community and professional organisations that can help us act.

First: Try using the <u>Ecological Rucksack</u>[21] calculator at home and/or at church.

Check out your church's progress against the UK "<u>Practical path</u>[22] to 'net zero carbon' for our churches".

Having used the calculator, can you work out a carbon budget for your house or church? Can you then estimate how much you need to reduce your carbon emissions to achieve a 6% reduction in a year? Do you think it is possible? If you are already solar-powered, then you are well on the way.

The <u>Australian Religious Response to Climate Change</u>[23] (ARRCC) is a multi-faith network taking action on the most pressing issue of our time. Visit their website and explore **Going "green" for householders and cool <u>lifestyle practices</u>[24] that will save you money.**

The <u>Season of Creation</u>[25] resources are well worth a look. Apart from a range of worship resources, there are also suggestions for action, primarily targeting diet, transport and energy consumption.

Season of Creation provides a link to <u>Living the Change</u>[26] that brings together people of faith and spirit, deeply grateful for the Earth. Living the Change wants our lives to reflect our values, avoiding excess and embracing sufficiency. Reducing the impact of our consumption is a spiritual challenge. By **<u>Living the Change</u>,** we engage this struggle with joy as part of our response to climate change. They highlight three areas and itemise the savings in emissions. Perhaps this can help you develop the carbon budget mentioned above.

21 https://ressourcen-rechner.de/calculator.php?lang=en#next

22 https://www.churchofengland.org/more/church-resources/churchcare/advice-and-guidance-church-buildings/practical-path-net-zero

23 https://www.arrcc.org.au/

24 https://www.arrcc.org.au/action_for_individual

25 https://seasonofcreation.org/about/

26 https://livingthechange.net/

Reducing ENERGY use

Moving towards renewable energy sources can save up to 1.6 tonnes of CO2 per year per person.

Eco-friendly TRANSPORT

Living car-free for a year saves 2.4 tonnes of greenhouse gas emissions, while each roundtrip transatlantic flight avoided saves an additional 1.6 tonnes.

Plant-based DIET

Eating a plant-based diet saves 0.8 tonnes of CO2 emissions per year. Plus, it is the most ethical approach, and helps improve health and well-being!

Third: Get serious and take the Eco Church[27] survey. Complete the unique online Eco Survey and find out how you compare with other churches in the caring for God's earth stakes.

The free online survey and supporting resources are designed to equip your church to express your care for God's world in your worship and teaching; in how you look after your buildings and land; in how you engage with your local community and in global campaigns; and in the personal lifestyles of your congregation.

> ▶ **View the Eco Church introductory 8 minute video** with Dr Ruth Valerio.

For a broader Australian perspective on action, see the excellent list available from the Climate Council: **12 CLIMATE ACTIONS TO MAKE AN IMPACT**[28]

In her inspiring resource, *The Future We Choose*, Christiana Figueres with co-author Tom Rivett-Carnac say the "time for doing what we can has passed. Each of us must now do what is necessary." They detail Ten Actions. Well worth reading.

Source: Living the Change

---

27 https://ecochurch.arocha.org.uk/overview-eco-church-scheme/

28 https://www.climatecouncil.org.au/12-climate-actions-make-impact/

Discussion:

- What first convinced you about the importance of climate change?

- What worries you most about climate change?

- Study 1 looked at links between the Coronavirus pandemic and climate change. Are there any lessons from the pandemic that should inform how we respond to climate change? Do you think action is needed urgently? Why?

- Have you discussed climate change with any people under 20 years of age? What were their perspectives?

Action

1. What has your church/community done to reduce its carbon emissions / carbon footprint?

   Did you try using the **Ecological Rucksack**[29] calculator at home and at Church?

   Have you checked your Church's progress against the UK "**Practical path**[30] to 'net zero carbon' for our churches"?

2. Can you arrange a meeting between your church/group and a local high school group or youth organisation active on climate change issues, to discuss common concerns and possible joint actions?

3. What have you been able to find out about what your state or local government is doing about climate change? Have they set any targets for emissions reduction?

29 https://ressourcen-rechner.de/calculator.php?lang=en#next

30 https://www.churchofengland.org/more/church-resources/churchcare/advice-and-guidance-church-buildings/practical-path-net-zero

Resources

Summer of Crisis[31], Climate Council 2019. Sydney.

Climate Council, 2016 https://www. climatecouncil.org.au/hottestyear2015

Video:

Interview with Christiana Figueres: See https://spckpublishing.co.uk/saying-yes-resources

An example from local government. What is happening in Newcastle?

https://www.youtube.com/watch?v=8HA2bx9IUSU&list=PLbIGOc-jExbTrTIrzvXl49OXR_DpMpO9BS&index-=6&t=21s

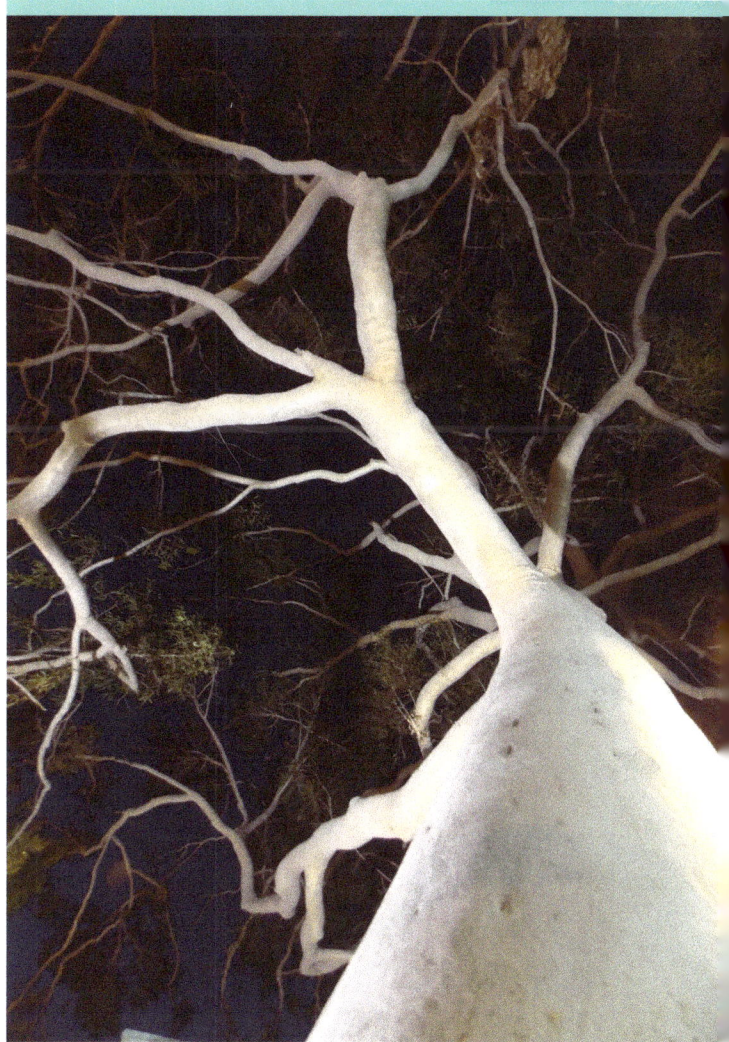

Photo credit: Russell Rollason

---

31 https://www.climatecouncil.org.au/resources/summer-of-crisis/

From Francis of Assisi and Scripture

"Let every creature in heaven, on earth, in the sea and in the depths, give praise, glory, honour and blessing to him who suffered so much, who has given and will give in the future every good, for he is our power and strength, who alone is good … and who alone is holy, worthy of praise and blessing through endless ages".
Francis of Assisi – 2nd Letter to the Faithful 61-62

"So God created humankind in his image, in the image of God he created them; male and female he created them. God blessed them … God saw everything that he had made, and indeed, it was very good."
Genesis 1:27, 31 NRSV

Reflection and Prayer

Creation is much more than something static, created in the past, as a background for human existence. We are intimately part of it, blessed by God with creative power. Creation is a web of complex relationships. Yet out of this complexity emerges a harmony of rich voices giving praise to God. Humankind has a privileged place in creation; may we accept the responsibility to use this privilege wisely, to be a blessing to all that God has made, that all may freely sing their praises to their creator.

Silence

Blessed are you, God of creation. You give us a world of infinite beauty and delight; a world in which nothing exists for itself alone and all are bound together as sisters and brothers. May we be wise stewards, using well the responsibility and all the creative powers of knowledge and skill you give us. May we, with all that you have made, find our place in the many voiced choir singing praise, glory, honour and blessing to you, the Source of all Being, who with Jesus Christ and the Holy Spirit is one God for ever.

Amen.

Study 3

Rediscovering our links with God's creation

STUDY 3: KEY POINTS

- Christian faith calls us to love one another and to be stewards of the earth.

- We are assured God will provide for us if we are faithful.

- What can we learn from First Peoples' link to land and creation?

- We must rediscover our mission to create a just, peaceful and sustainable future for all.

- How can we be "hope tellers"?

Watch the video (4.45 mins): Archbishop Winston Halapua, Diocese of Polynesia, prays and gives thanks for the Moana Ocean.
https://acen.anglicancommunion.org/resources/anglican-bishops-for-climate-justice.aspx

We are part of Creation

As Christians we see ourselves as part of Creation.

In Genesis 3:19 we are reminded that human beings are made from the land and return to the land. In Genesis 2:15, God committed the care of creation to us. We have the responsibility to serve and sustain the land.

Anglican Bishops from across the globe gathered in South Africa in June 2015, to reflect on the 'unprecedented climate crisis' and the deep impacts of 'climate injustice and environmental degradation'. The Bishops recognised that 'the Church must urgently find its collective moral voice'.

In the statement adopted by the gathering, the Bishops "held fast to our hope in the promises of God, the one who will restore all creation (Romans 8:18-25) and who will make all things new (2 Corinthians 5:17; Revelation 21:5)".

The Bishops affirmed the climate change crisis as the most urgent moral issue of our day that "calls for a profound change of heart and mind. In keeping with 1 Corinthians 12:26, the connection between lifestyle and use of resources in one part of the world affects the whole world. They discerned a call to revitalize our human vocation that refuses to leave some poor and others rich, and to rediscover our joy and awe in the wonders of God's creation (Psalm 96: 11-12)".

In his introduction to the 2020 Lenten Studies, titled "Say Yes to Life", the Archbishop of Canterbury, Justin Welby, comments:

"Sadly, Christians have not always given God's creation the reverence it deserves. The Old Testament offers us a picture of human beings as intimately linked to their environment, where their actions have a profound effect on the land, and they are held responsible for it".

Photo credit: Russell Rollason

"It is of the utmost importance that we now stand in solidarity together, repenting of our sins towards our earth and committing to face our responsibilities as God's people. As people of faith, we cannot just say what we believe. We are obliged to live out the life that Christ calls us to live, to care for our neighbours, for the creatures and the creation that God has so generously given us".

The Archbishop calls us "to rebuild our relationship with our planet so that we might rebuild our relationship with its creator".

Goals for a new earth

Have you often reflected on the values that we, as Christians, offer the world? How do you explain God's vision for the future of the world?

Around 2700 years ago, the prophet Isaiah set out a vision for new heaven and a new earth:

"For I am about to create new heavens and a new earth; the former things shall not be remembered or come to mind.
But be glad and rejoice for ever in what I am creating;"
Isaiah 65:17

Photo credit: Russell Rollason

Isaiah spells out a simple but profound vision for a better world. Reflected by Jesus in the Lord's Prayer, this inspiring vision of a new earth is repeated daily around the world: 'your kingdom come on earth as it is in heaven'.

Isaiah outlines (Is 65:8-25) what a good life would look like: health for young and old; the right to secure housing; the right to fulfilling work and to enjoy the fruits of our labour; and peace and security in national borders. Similar goals are reflected in contemporary language in the United Nations Sustainable Development Goals (SDGs). Each day when we say the Lord's Prayer, we join our prayers for this simple vision to be realized in solidarity with those of the Church across the world.

We believe all are created in the image of God and the earth's resources are to be shared amongst all people. We share a vision of a world based on love: a world where we care for our neighbours, especially those living on the margins of society, and live in peace with each other and with the environment.

But the god of Mammon still tempts us today with material possessions beyond our wildest dreams. The price of limitless consumerism is plain to see – environmental destruction, rising temperatures, air and water pollution, droughts, floods, bushfires, wild storms, rising sea levels, and the loss of millions of species of animals. If we want a kinder, gentler world, we will have to fight the dark side with its rapacious greed and inequality.

In our craving for 'things', we have lost our links to the ecosystem. We have been lax in caring for God's creation.

Some observers point to Australia's Black Summer of bushfires as a sign of our failure to care for God's creation. In the discussion and reflection that followed the bushfires, many Australians have come to understand that uncontrolled wildfires were not common before European settlement. Our eyes have been opened to the different way Aboriginal Australians managed the land. They used fire to sustain the vegetation and wildlife, not to destroy it. And they did so for more than 60,000 years.

Our responsibility to the land

In rebuilding our relationship with the Creation, there is much we can learn from Torres Strait Islander and Aboriginal Australian Christians.

Rainbow Spirit Theology[32] observes that the God of the Scriptures is known as the Creator Spirit, who speaks through the land.

The following quotes from *Rainbow Spirit Theology* provide a glimpse into a deep spirituality that has flourished in this land.

"Traditional Aboriginal people have a deep sense of responsibility for the welfare of the land entrusted to our care. The Creator Spirit is the true landowner, and human beings are like trustees, responsible to the Creator Spirit for the care of this land".

"Our Aboriginal culture was already spiritual, more overtly spiritual than the European culture of those who invaded Australia. God was already speaking to us through the law revealed in the land".

"Aboriginal Christians do not understand the Gospel in a narrow sense which focuses exclusively on rescuing souls from personal sin and arranging their transfer to heaven. Christ came to redeem lives, communities and, ultimately, all creation from the forces of evil at work in the world".

Photo credit: Russell Rollason

"I feel a deep spiritual connection with the land. When that connection is broken, I suffer. Has Christ come to break that connection or to restore it?"[33]

Aboriginal Anglican priest the Rev'd Glenn Loughrey in a reflection of Pentecost observed: "We, each, hear the Spirit in the land we live in, and it is unique, diverse, and we discover it is already there, embedded all around us. We begin to see, hear and act in sync with what has been there all the time.

"This is where our sense of justice comes from – we discover that the Spirit is just-us and if the spirit enlivens us then we are to treat all as just-us, not different, less than, inferior to, objects to be used but they are just-us and therefore deserve the respect and fairness we say is found in Christ who is in us," says Glenn.[34]

32 Rainbow Spirit Theology: Towards an Australian Aboriginal Theology, by the Rainbow Spirit Elders. Harper Collins Religious, 1997

33 Ibid

34 Loughrey, Glenn. 'Homeland Calling: Let the revolution begin.' Blog 2020. https://www.redshoeswalking.net/homeland-calling-let-the-revolution-begin/

A Mark of Mission

The worldwide Anglican Communion accepted the Marks of Mission as originally articulated by the Anglican Consultative Council in 1984. The fifth mark is "to strive to safeguard the integrity of creation and sustain and renew the life of the Earth". The Anglican Board of Mission - Australia has translated this mark to "Protect, care for and renew life on our planet".

Following the 10th Assembly of the World Council of Churches (WCC) in Busan in 2013, a "Roadmap for Congregations, Communities, and Churches for an Economy of Life and Ecological Justice" invited Christians worldwide to join a pilgrimage towards an Economy of Life and climate justice.

Preparations for the 11th WCC assembly in 2021 have recognised the Kairos moment in history in which we find ourselves. "The task ahead is immense and will require decades of dedication. The urgency of the situation implies that a comprehensive response cannot be delayed. The next decade will be decisive to allow the Earth a time of rest." The call is out for the WCC assembly next year to declare a "Decade for the Healing of Creation".

Climate Change for children

Children are increasingly asking about climate change. If you wish to start a discussion with children, there are some great resources available from the Anglican Communion Environment Network (ACEN).[35]

In particular have a look at the highly successful "Let there be stuff"[36] video and study.

Psalm 24 reminds us, "The earth is the Lord's, and everything in it, the world, and all who live in it; for he founded it on the seas and established it on the waters." Each of us has a responsibility to live a life that cares for God's world and its creatures.

35 https://acen.anglicancommunion.org/resources/children,-youth-and-the-environment.aspx

36 http://www.aco.org/media/285783/Let-there-be-stuff.pdf

Discussion

Two quotes from *A Gospel of Hope* by Walter Brueggemann:

"We have prayed that God's will may be done on earth as it is in heaven (Matt 6:10). We have imagined how it is in heaven and have petitioned that the earth should be the same. Even in our praying, however, we did not know that the earth could be transformed. We believed that our cities are hopeless, that our policies and practices must be endlessly filled with poison and death. All of that destructiveness, however, has run out of steam and authority. A Newness is coming beyond our power to speak or to start. It is a newness rooted in God's power, now coming to embodiment in human, earthly, public form."

"Hope is the deep religious conviction that God has not quit."

• How can we become 'hope tellers' that break the spell of despair?

• Brueggemann has also said that "Hope is grounded in memories." What do you think he means by this? Can you name some things that people hoped for in the past that are now a reality?

Action

The gathering of Bishops in South Africa in 2015 agreed to encourage Anglicans everywhere to:

• Join in prayer and fasting for climate justice on the first day of each month as an integral part of life and worship.

• Implement energy conservation measures in church buildings and move to renewable energy sources as quickly as possible.

• Take measures to conserve, recycle and collect water around church buildings and properties.

The **Roadmap for Congregations**,[37] *Communities, and Churches for an Economy of Life and Ecological Justice* invites congregations, communities and churches to join a pilgrimage for an Economy of Life and climate justice, to commit to make changes in the way we live, to share successful ideas and to encourage one another. It introduces a five-step programme to change the way we deal with the economy and our ecological surroundings. Join the pilgrimage on a journey for change.

37 https://www.oikoumene.org/en/resources/documents/wcc-programmes/diakonia/economy-of-life/roadmap-for-congregations-communities-and-churches-for-an-economy-of-life-and-ecological-justice?search-term=Roadmap

Resources

Say Yes to Life, by Ruth Valerio. *SPCK* London, *2019*

Rainbow Spirit Theology: *Towards an Australian Aboriginal Theology,* by the Rainbow Spirit Elders. Harper Collins Religious, 1997

THE WORLD IS OUR HOST:[38] A CALL TO URGENT ACTION FOR CLIMATE JUSTICE 2015

Roadmap for Congregations, Communities, and Churches for an Economy of Life and Ecological Justice. World Council of Churches, 2019

Walter Brueggemann, A Gospel of Hope. Westminister John Knox Press, 2018

Two podcasts of HOPE

1. St Paul's Anglican Church, Beaconsfield, WA – a series of interviews after a scene-setter from Professor Peter Newman then Dr Fiona Stanley and others

   http://stpaulsbeaconsfield.org.au/church-events

2. Fifth Estate podcast with Peter Newman, Professor of Sustainability, Curtin University. Finishes with the 'diamonds' vision from Revelation.

   https://thefifthestate.us5.list-manage.com/track/click?u=c4d1e2f51d67481aaefde7be9&id=d4bf197e39&e=a0fcc5e41c

Several videos are available on the ACEN[39] website.

---

38 http://acen.anglicancommunion.org/media/148818/The-World-is-our-Host-FINAL-TEXT.pdf

39 https://acen.anglicancommunion.org/

From Francis of Assisi and Scripture

"Consider, O human being, in what great excellence the Lord God has placed you, for he created and formed you to the image of his beloved Son according to the body and to his likeness according to the Spirit."

Francis of Assisi – Admonitions 5:1

"It was fitting that God, for whom and through whom all things exist, in bringing many children to glory, should make the pioneer of their salvation perfect through sufferings. For the one who sanctifies and those who are sanctified all have one Father. For this reason Jesus is not ashamed to call them brothers and sisters, saying, 'I will proclaim your name to my brothers and sisters, in the midst of the congregation I will praise you.' And again, 'I will put my trust in him.' And again, 'Here am I and the children whom God has given me.'

Hebrews 2:10-13 NRSV

Reflection and Prayer

We live in the world God created and redeems, the world in which God calls us to be the hands, the feet, the eyes of Jesus—that we may look out with the love of God and do God's will. To grow in the image of Christ is not just an individual task, but one we do together with our brothers and sisters as we care for all that God gives in creation.

Silence

Blessed are you, God of humankind. You place us in excellence, yet we so often fail to reach the promise you hold out to us. When we fall, may we not be discouraged, but stand again. Be with us in our lives, our actions, our words, as we minister to creation the presence of Christ, our Saviour.

Amen.

Study 4

Climate Change: changing behaviour

STUDY 4: KEY POINTS

STUDY 4: KEY POINTS

- Recognising the challenge to change behaviour.

- How can the Christian community provide a safe place for the lonely, the anxious and the fearful?

- Climate grief and intergenerational responsibility.

- Youth have little voice in shaping their future.

"You are failing us, but the young people are starting to understand your betrayal. The eyes of all future generations are upon you and if you choose to fail us, I say: We will never forgive you".
Greta Thunberg

The issues

Climate Change is a global challenge. It casts its spell over all and demands a response at the personal, community, national and international levels.

National and international action

As an international mission and development cooperation agency, ABM draws on the experiences and activities of partner communities in the Pacific, Asia and Africa to share stories of climate change impacts and the efforts of local communities to adapt. In particular, ABM gives high priority to supporting the lives and livelihoods of the peoples of the South Pacific.

Australia has signed the Paris Accord that sets out a plan to avoid dangerous climate change by limiting global warming to well below 2°C. Consequently, Australia has a responsibility to halve our emissions by 2030 to achieve the Paris target. All Christians should contribute to debate and advocacy activities to ensure Australia honours its international commitments, especially to the Paris Accord, Agenda 21 and the Sustainable Development Goals, referred to as the **Zero carbon Zero poverty** agenda.

As you will see through these studies and in the links provided, there has been real progress in addressing climate change in Australia. For example, all 8 Australian states and territories have net zero emission targets in place. Local governments around Australia have practical programs to reduce greenhouse gas emissions through cutting energy consumption, and improving public transport, for example. Such progress is to be celebrated and encouraged.

As one of the world's highest per capita carbon emitters and its leading exporter of coal, Australia should be a leader in climate change action. We need to urge the Federal Government to increase its commitments under the Paris Agreement, to adopt an energy plan to phase out fossil fuels and to encourage a rapid increase in investments in solar and wind generation and storage in Australia.

A **survey of public opinion**[40] taken soon after the bushfires by researchers at the University of Canberra found four out of five of those surveyed thought climate change was 'somewhat serious' to 'extremely serious'.

Photo credit: Russell Rollason

40 https://www.canberra.edu.au/research/faculty-research-centres/nmrc/digital-news-report-australia-2020

Young people expressed much more concern than older generations, and city dwellers expressed more concern than regional and rural Australians.

Key concerns identified by the researchers were that 8% of Australians see climate change as not at all serious (double the global average of 3%) and 15% of respondents said they don't pay any attention to news about climate change. The researchers commented that the disinterest of a significant section of the community reflects the difficulty in gaining political momentum for action.[41] Changing public attitudes is critical for climate change action.

Climate Change requires behavioural change

Addressing climate change is an essential and urgent task if we are to have a chance of restoring a safe climate for humans and other species, according to the Australian Psychological Society. "Because climate change is caused by human behaviour, threatens human health and wellbeing, and requires profound changes in human behaviour to bring about solutions, it is as much a psychological and social problem as it is an environmental or ecological mega-disaster."[42]

Photo credit: Russell Rollason

The insights of psychologists and other social scientists into how people are responding to climate change are therefore critically important. The more we understand the psychology of how people are responding to climate change, the better we can help ourselves and others to overcome barriers of inaction.

"***The Climate Change Empowerment Handbook***:[43] *Psychological strategies to tackle climate change*" contains 'best practice' insights from psychological science to help people come to terms and cope with the profound implications of climate change. It provides sound advice on how to stay engaged with the problem, see where own behaviour plays a part, and how to participate in speedy societal change to restore a safe climate. The Handbook offers eight insights that make the acronym **A.C.T.I.V.A.T.E.**[44] The APS aims to ACTIVATE the public into more effectively engaging with the challenge of climate change!

41 Fisher, Caroline and Park, Sara. The number of climate deniers in Australia is more than double the global average, new survey finds in The Conversation. 16 June 2020

42 The Climate Change Empowerment Handbook. 2018 Australian Psychological Society p3

43 https://www.psychology.org.au/for-the-public/Psychology-topics/Climate-change-psychology

44 https://www.psychology.org.au/getmedia/b2304d9c-64d4-40a6-b063-3014128ec740/ACTIVATE-climate-change.pdf?utm_medium=Promo-Tile&utm_source=website

The Climate Change Empowerment Handbook highlights the dilemma that "we *know*, yet at the same time we seem to *not know* enough to act". In a world of 'fake news', self-serving interests and herd mentality it is hardly surprising that this dilemma arises. The psychologists call it 'cognitive biases'. It manifests in a range of ways. These include reluctance to accept scientific advice and downplaying the risks — after all, some say, we inhale carbon dioxide in every breath we take, so how can it be so bad for the earth? Also, how we see the problem depends on our values, beliefs and worldviews. Our biases shape how we see the world around us.

If you would like to explore these issues further, see *the Climate Change Empowerment Handbook*, beginning at page 4.

Photo credit: Russell Rollason

Anxiety and uncertainty: how can we help?

Anxiety, stress and depression are unfortunately too common in our society. In the wake of the Coronavirus, calls to mental health counselling services, such as Beyond Blue and Lifeline, have increased significantly.

The World Health Organisation recently warned of a mental health crisis as people around the world deal with the anxiety and loneliness caused by the Coronavirus and subsequent social distancing measures. In a report to the UN, the WHO mental health department warned of serious mental illness among children, young people and medical workers. It pointed to the fear, the isolation, the uncertainty and the economic turmoil as likely cause for psychological distress.[45]

Following the Australian bushfires, there was a similar spike in people seeking help for mental illness. How do we help people who have lost everything both materially and spiritually? How do people start over?

45 Global report: WHO says Covid-19 'may never go away' and warns of mental health crisis. The Guardian 14 May 20.

Listen to young people

Climate change anxiety has added dimensions. Children and youth have little voice in shaping their future. Decisions that will affect their lives are taken by parents, local leaders, governments, global economic decision makers, and by the captains of global corporations with enormous resources and purely commercial interests.

Swedish activist Greta Thunberg, who started the global student movement, effectively made the point when she told world leaders at the United Nations:

You have stolen my dreams and my childhood with your empty words and yet I'm one of the lucky ones. People are suffering. People are dying. Entire ecosystems are collapsing. We are in the beginning of a mass extinction and all you can talk about is money and fairy tales of eternal economic growth. How dare you!

Health researchers report that parents are dealing with inconsolably anxious children, fearing for their future after learning about climate breakdown in the classroom; psychiatrists are reporting growing numbers of patients frozen in anger and anxiety for their lack of control over what is to come for our planet, themselves and their children; farmers in Australia are driven to suicide by climate change-influenced droughts; youth mental health charities are reporting their users lose sleep worrying about environmental and political issues. The case is building, and it's time to take it seriously.[46]

The growing trend of people seeking mental health support to process the implications of climate change has led professional bodies – such as the American Psychological Association in the USA and the UK Council for Psychotherapy – to raise awareness, and consider how best to manage these emerging mental health needs. In 2018, the Yale Program on Climate Change Communications made a study of adults in the United States. It found that, of those who accept climate change is happening, 62% feel afraid and helpless.[47]

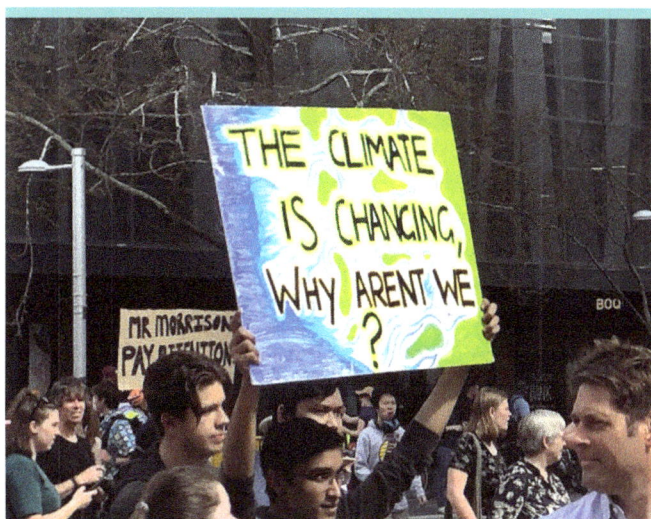

Photo credit: Russell Rollason

46 Lawrance, Emma, Mental Health Innovations Fellow at Imperial's Institute of Global Health Innovation, blogs

47 https://climatecommunication.yale.edu/wp-content/uploads/2019/01/Climate-Change-American-Mind-December-2018.pdf

Climate Grief

Australian singer-songwriter Missy Higgins says climate grief has been at the heart of her most recent songs, released on the 'Solastalgia'[48] album. In a recent ABC Radio National interview, Missy explained that "when we were thinking of having another child, I was feeling quite heavily the responsibility of bringing another human being into the world … because they are going to inherit this really unpredictable world we are creating for them. …

"Then I realised that what I'm feeling is grief and anxiety, and I need to deal with this", she explained.

"I wrote an article about climate anxiety after having a kid, but the response I got was quite amazing and it made me realise how many other people are having this anxiety at the moment. … I'm actively trying to right this wrong, and I can sleep better at night, even if I think it's probably only a really small difference," said Missy Higgins.

Photo credit: Genex Kidston Solar Farm, <u>https://www.genexpower.com.au/</u>

48 Solastalgia: , simply put, is "the homesickness you have when you are still at home". See https://theconversation.com/the-age-of-solastalgia-8337

Intergenerational responsibilities

COVID-19 has underlined the intergenerational aspect of the two crises. The virus has targeted old people but it is the young who have been hit hardest by the economic shutdown. So much so that some argue the health of the old shouldn't have received priority over the health of the economy.

There are multiple reasons why the young bear a heavy economic burden in this crisis. Many are in casual jobs, and in sectors most harmed, such as hospitality. Also, people beginning their careers during a downturn take longer to 'catch up' financially with those who commenced in good times. And younger people will be the taxpayers of the future as the country deals with the debt.[49]

When it comes to paying off the debt, it will largely fall on young people. They not only have to deal with losing their job now, but will also have to deal with climate change and pay the debts incurred by the past generation. Intergenerational fairness does suggest that an early start should be made to paying off the debt, and the current older generation must contribute.

It is not surprising that many young people are anxious about the future. We have a particular duty of care for young people who will inherit our failings.

How to talk about mental health

As the impacts of climate change become more intense, our churches / community will need to be prepared to help people struggling with anxiety and uncertainty. While some may need the help of health professionals, others may simply be looking for someone to talk to about the challenges they are facing and perhaps seeking guidance on where they might find further help. But how can we prepare?

Understanding how to talk about mental health is an important skill. Many people feel uncomfortable and unprepared, and this can mean the conversation never starts at all. Mental Health First Aid courses teach people the skills to feel confident about what to do next if someone says "No, I'm not okay."

For more information: **mental health first aid**[50] and the national **R U OK**[51] activities and resources.

49 Breunig, Bob. Tax and Transfer Unit, ANU. Quoted in Grattan on Friday: Intergenerational fairness puts COVID-19 obligation on older people. The Conversation 16 April 2020.

50 https://mhfa.com.au/news/2019-09-12/54693/conversation-could-change-life-and-right-skills-can-make-difference

51 https://www.ruok.org.au/how-to-ask

Discussion

- What's happened since your last discussion group meeting? Any news to report? Any new discoveries? Anything you saw or heard during the week that has influenced your thinking?

- How can you engage with young people in your area to discuss issues of climate change and find reasons for hope?

- How do you think the Church can best enter into a discussion with people who are not convinced about the need to act now on climate change?

- How important are mental and spiritual issues in the global fight to reduce carbon emissions?

Action

What has been your experience in climate change discussions? Have you found it difficult to raise the issue? Which issues have become barriers in your discussions?

Have you or your parish met any young people struggling with anxiety about climate change? Have you shared discussion time with them? How best might you help young people with anxiety to seek assistance?

Are there people in your parish / community trained in Mental Health First Aid? Are others interested in taking a course in Mental Health First Aid?

Do you have a ready list of the Mental Health services available in your area? Have you ever spoken to them?

Resources

Climate Change and Psychology: https://www.psychology.org.au/for-the-public/Psychology-topics/Climate-change-psychology

The Climate Change Empowerment Handbook: https://www.psychology.org.au/for-the-public/Psychology-topics/Climate-change-psychology/Climate-change

RUOK Conversation Corner: https://www.ruok.org.au/how-to-ask

Images credit: RUOK

From Francis of Assisi and Scripture

"Most high, glorious God, enlighten the darkness of my heart and give me true faith, certain hope, and perfect charity, sense and knowledge, Lord, that I may carry out your holy and true command."
Francis of Assisi – Prayer before the Crucifix

"May the God of hope fill you with all joy and peace in believing, so that you may abound in hope by the power of the Holy Spirit."
Romans 8:13 NRSV

Reflection and Prayer

With Francis we too can pray for the faith, hope, love, sense and knowledge we need to carry out what God asks of us. Hope gives us the vision that lifts our eyes above what seems impossible. Without hope, the problems we face are insurmountable, a mountain we cannot climb. With hope we can see over that mountain to our distant goal and trace the steps that will finally take us there.

Silence

Blessed are you, God of hope. You inspire us to seek what seems high and distant. You help us start on the journey. You show that each step taken makes the goal closer. When the path closes in and we cannot see our steps, you bring us back again to the vision of that goal. Be with us as we journey, that in our striving we may know our Companion, Jesus Christ with us.

Amen.

Study 5

Grounds for Hope

STUDY 5: KEY POINTS

- Pointing to the signs of hope and the gathering momentum.

- Building community understanding and commitment to face the changes ahead; reassuring the anxious and unsure.

- Sharing the burden of change and revealing the better world ahead.

- Making sure we leave no one behind.

Fourth Century North African theologian and pioneer of Christianity, Augustine of Hippo wrote:

"Hope has two beautiful daughters, their names are anger and courage. Anger that things are the way they are, and courage to see that they do not remain as they are."

Around Australia and around the world, people are realising that we need to face three converging crises: the COVID-19 pandemic and the resulting economic recession; the climate emergency; and extreme inequality.

The challenges are significant but signs of hope abound. Momentum towards a zero emissions sustainable world is gathering pace, although hurdles remain. There is a real and present climate for change.

Green New Deal

In the 1930s, then President of the United States Franklin D. Roosevelt enacted 'The New Deal'. It was a series of programmes, public work projects and financial reforms aimed at restoring the American economy and reviving a sense of hope in the American people after the Great Depression.

Inspired by the New Deal of the 1930's, politicians around the world have been proposing measures to address climate change and inequality under the theme of the Green New Deal.

In February 2019, Democrat Representative Alexandria Ocasio-Cortez from New York introduced a Green New Deal[52] resolution in the US Congress. It laid out a grand plan for tackling climate change. It called on the federal government to wean the United States from fossil fuels and curb planet-warming greenhouse gas emissions across the economy. It also aimed to guarantee new high-paying jobs in clean energy industries.[53]

In Europe, seventeen climate and environment ministers adopted a European Green New Deal[54] statement. They agreed that "the world is facing an unprecedented crisis". While the focus was on fighting the

Photo credit: Suzlon wind farm in Hallett, South Australia

pandemic, they urged recovery plans for "sustainable progress and prosperity."[55]

They also agreed that "we must not lose sight of the persisting climate and ecological crisis. Building momentum to fight this battle has to stay high on the political agenda."

In the UK, the Green New Deal[56] is a community-led plan to secure a safe climate and fairer society, by transforming the economy. It is not a single policy, but an ambitious programme of policies, investment and regulation. These recognise that the causes of the climate and inequality crises are the same. The Green New Deal must be international – supporting all peoples and countries to rapidly decarbonise and tackle inequality, while ensuring the UK does its fair share to address climate breakdown.[57]

The International Renewable Energy Agency (IRENA) has outlined a path to stability[58] and prosperity based on the adoption of renewable energy for a low-carbon future.

52 https://www.nytimes.com/2019/02/21/climate/green-new-deal-questions-answers.html

53 What is the Green New Deal? https://www.nytimes.com/2019/02/21/climate/green-new-deal-questions-answers.html

54 https://www.climatechangenews.com/2020/04/09/europe-an-green-deal-must-central-resilient-recovery-covid-19/

55 European Green Deal: https://www.climatechangenews.com/2020/04/09/european-green-deal-must-central-resilient-recovery-covid-19/

56 https://www.greennewdealuk.org/

57 The Green New Deal https://www.greennewdealuk.org/

58 https://www.irena.org/DigitalArticles/2020/Apr/Renewable_energy_for_a_low_carbon_future

A vision for Australia

Eminent Australian economist Professor Ross Garnaut outlined a vision for Australia as an energy "Superpower" in his book of the same name, published just before the coronavirus. Garnaut foresees that, if we rise to the challenge of climate change, we "will emerge as a global superpower in energy, low-carbon industry and absorption of carbon in the landscape".

The cost of moving to renewable energy is much debated. But it is clear that the cost of not moving will be far greater. Low-carbon electricity will be cheaper and will give us major new export opportunities, according to Garnaut. Hotter and drier conditions in rural areas will leave farmers struggling to make ends meet, and the demise of coal mining will further weaken rural economies. But Professor Garnaut sees rural areas getting a whole new source of income and activity created by the world's move to renewable energy in the regions.

He also highlights the opportunity for Australia to export renewable energy. This will be by exporting electricity through submarine cables or exporting hydrogen made with renewable energy. Large scale renewable energy also opens up opportunities for refining minerals near mine sites, rather than exporting mineral ores overseas for processing.[59]

Recover, Rebuild, Renew

In May 2020, 15 Australian community sector organisations, led by Australian Conversation Foundation, joined to encourage governments to bolster their jobs and recovery strategies. They urged measures to reduce emissions and accelerate successful energy transitions across all Australia's regions and economic sectors. The group pointed to the opportunity for investment in better energy efficiency and energy management. Coinciding with the release of the statement, ACF also published a report, **"Recover, Rebuild, Renew"**.[60] It outlines "a new path that builds our economy, helps fix the climate crisis and creates a fairer, healthier and more resilient Australia for all, including our children and grandchildren".[61]

59 Gittins, Ross. Zero net carbon choice: do we want to be losers or winners? Sydney Morning Herald. 29/1/20

60 https://www.acf.org.au/recover_rebuild_renew_lets_make_things_right_for_people_and_our_country

61 Australian Conservation Foundation. Recover, Rebuild Renew. https://www.acf.org.au/recover_rebuild_renew_lets_make_things_right_for_people_and_our_country

We have found that technology has achieved significant progress since 2014, often faster than was expected

New renewables now **cheaper** than new fossil fuel generation

Battery costs per kilowatt-hour **80% cheaper** than in 2010

10-storey office tower built in timber in Brisbane

3 million EVs driven in the world

The **share price** of Beyond Meat grew more than 700% in the 3 months following its release

1- and 2-person **electric planes** are beginning to enter the market

Source: ClimateWorks Australia, Decarbonisation Futures

Decarbonisation

Climate Works Australia published a comprehensive report, **"Decarbonisation Futures"**. It explains why the stimulus to recover from the pandemic will need exactly the sort of actions that are needed to address the climate crisis.[62]

"Decarbonisation Futures" examines the potential for emission reducing innovations across Australia's entire economy. The summary of the report is presented in easy to understand charts and diagrams. It shows how rapid progress and plummeting cost of green technology provide an unprecedented opportunity for Australia to move to a net zero emissions economy by 2050.

Green Steel

One of the proposals for renewal in former coal mining regions is the development of new hydrogen-powered steel-making. This will increase the processing of Australian iron ore in this country.

Report from the Grattan Institute[63] suggests using Australia's plentiful wind and solar resources to make energy-intensive 'green' commodities. It says this could create tens of thousands of jobs in regions that now employ tens of thousands of coal miners and other 'carbon workers'. These are the very workers whose jobs are threatened by global efforts to cut carbon emissions.[64]

Green steel uses hydrogen, produced from water or gas using renewable energy, to replace metallurgical coal used in iron ore smelting. Australia's extensive wind and solar energy resources mean we can make hydrogen, and therefore green steel, more cheaply than countries such as Japan, Korea, and Indonesia.

"Capturing about 6.5 per cent of the global steel market would generate about $65 billion in annual export revenue and could create 25,000 manufacturing jobs in Queensland and NSW," states the Grattan Institute report. 'Green steel' could help make Australia a renewable energy superpower. It represents the best opportunity for exports and job creation in key regions.

62 Decarbonisation Futures https://www.climateworksaustralia.org/project/decarbonisation-futures/

63 https://grattan.edu.au/report/start-with-steel/

64 Wood, Tony et al, Start with Steel, Grattan Institute, Melbourne. 2019 https://grattan.edu.au/report/start-with-steel/

Grounds for hope

Grounds for hope lie in the thoughtful and practical ideas offered by individuals and think tanks across the globe. Information from international organisations, universities and research bodies around the world is available on the internet. See the **Annex of Hope** in this booklet for some snippets.

To gift our grandchildren a liveable and sustainable world, we must avoid catastrophic climate change by making sure global temperatures do not increase by more than 1.5°C.

To achieve this target, we must cut carbon emissions by half this decade (2020s), by half next decade (2030s), and stop using fossil fuels altogether to reach net zero emissions by 2050. We must cut carbon emissions by around 6-7% each year in order to halve emissions by 2030.

The goal is achievable. The technology is available. **What is missing is the political will to make the change.** This is where citizens like us become critical. We must build that political commitment by persuading our friends and neighbours as well as members of parliament at State and Federal level to act now on climate change.

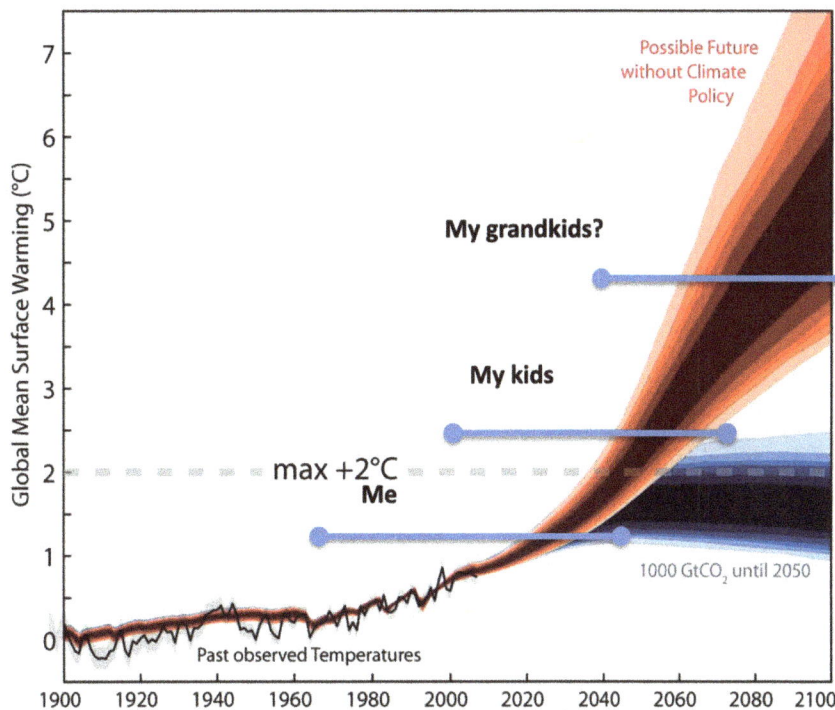

Source: Adapted from Prof Lesley Hughes, Climate Council

The critical but scarce resource: political will

Six bricks for building a climate for change:

1. It is important to take action at home and at Church. Have a look at the Climate Council's suggestions, including **Home Energy Efficiency Tips.**[65] We are all in this together, so try sharing progress with others from your group and with friends. Taking action at home builds our credibility to ask others to take action, too.

2. How can we strengthen the national dialogue and commitment to create a fairer, more just, zero-carbon zero-poverty world for all? Are there other groups / organisations that you are involved in? Could you encourage them to discuss the issues?

   A dialogue means engaging with people face-to-face to help them think through the change, understand why it is necessary, and to discover hope for the future. If we want to convince people of the need to change, we need to talk with them face-to-face.

3. We need to reduce carbon dioxide emissions by 6-7% each year. We need to plan how we / our family / our Church are going to reduce our emissions. The International Energy Agency estimates that global CO2 emissions will fall by 8% in 2020, largely due to the sharp drop in demand for coal and oil (mainly because few planes are flying). This gives us a good idea of the scale of change that is needed. But after COVID-19, emissions may rebound quickly unless changes are made.

   Did you try using the **Ecological Rucksack**[66] calculator at home and at Church during Study 2?

   If you have not done so, check out your Church's progress against the UK "**Practical path**"[67] to 'net zero carbon' for our churches".

   On a broader scale, communities can now get a free **Snapshot**[68] of their carbon emissions. This is the first national tool providing community wide greenhouse gas profiles for every council across Australia.

4. Are there groups in your area working on a fairer, greener future? Can you or your church offer support? What about getting your community started as a Zero Carbon Community? Tools and guidance are available at **Zero Carbon Communities**[69].

5. Which industries will be most affected by the move to a zero carbon future in your region / local area? How will we all share the costs of the shift to a zero carbon future? Who is planning for new jobs for those displaced by the shift to a zero carbon future? Research by **Beyond Zero Carbon**[70]

65 https://www.climatecouncil.org.au/home-energy-efficiency-tips-save-money-emissions/

66 https://ressourcen-rechner.de/calculator.php?lang=en#next

67 https://www.churchofengland.org/more/church-resources/churchcare/advice-and-guidance-church-buildings/practical-path-net-zero

68 https://snapshotclimate.com.au/

69 https://bze.org.au/home/zero-carbon-communities/

70 https://bze.org.au/research/

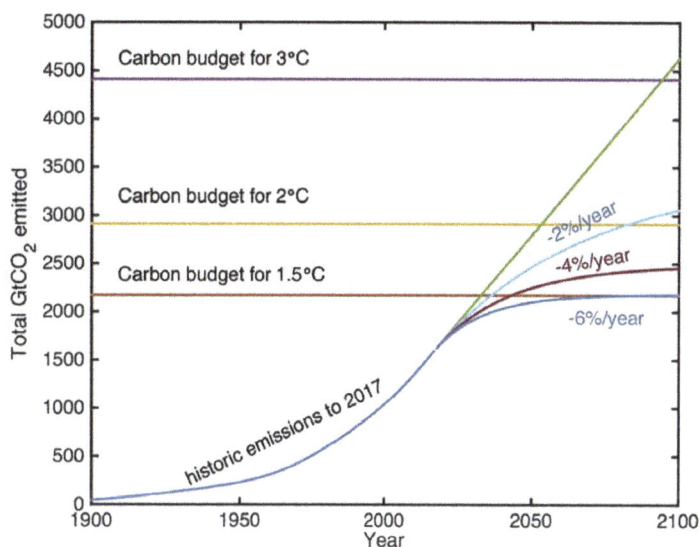

This graph shows different emission pathways and when the world is expected to reach global average temperatures of 1.5° or 2° above pre-industrial levels.

Source: Mc Lachlan, Robert, Climate explained. (drawn from the Global Carbon Project) The Conversation, 29 July 2020.

is a helpful and inspiring starting point. Can you find other groups looking at future jobs to replace the carbon intensive ones of today such as coal mining?

6. The final step in building political will is sharing the groundswell of public concern with members of parliament, from all political parties. Representing the area where you live, there will be local councillors, at least one State MP (in some States there will also be a State Upper House representative), one Federal MP and at least one Federal Senator. To find your federal electorate, go to **aec.gov.au**

Arrange a meeting with your parliamentary representatives. A meeting would preferably be no more than 5 people, perhaps including people from other local groups. Try to engage in a discussion, not just a litany of requests and no demands. You want your MP to support the case you are presenting. If your meeting goes for an hour and all leave feeling heard and understood, you have done well. You might also invite one of your representatives to a discussion at your church.

Take a photo and report back to your group. Then plan your next step. After the first meeting, the subsequent ones will be much easier!

To conclude, a quote from Christiana Figueres in her inspiring book with Tom Rivett-Carnac, "The Future We Choose":

"We want you to know two things.

"First, even at this late hour we still have a choice about our future, and therefore every action we take from this moment forward counts.

"Second, we are capable of making the right choices about our own destiny. We are not doomed to a devastating future, and humanity is not flawed and incapable of responding to big problems if we act.

"Future generations will most likely look back to this moment as the single most important turning point for action."

Let's not miss the opportunity that the current climate for change offers.

Discussion

- What's happened since your last discussion group meeting? Any news to report? Any new discoveries? Anything you saw or heard during the week that has influenced your thinking?

- What gives you hope that the world will avoid catastrophic climate change and keep temperature rise to 1.5°C or less?

- How best can we use the power of our faith to support emission reductions?

- Which group in your region is most likely to be adversely affected by climate change? How will climate change affect them?

- Have you spoken to people who will lose their jobs as a result of climate change or actions to reduce emissions? Can you meet with a group of these people?

- What can be done in your region to ensure the burden of emissions reductions falls on all, and not just on those who lose their jobs? Are there any groups addressing this issue?

- How can we make real the hope that lies at the heart of the Gospels?

Action

1. All 8 Australian states and territories have net zero emissions targets in place. What is your state/territory's commitment and what is the deadline date? Is there any way your Church can help achieve this target?

2. Have you undertaken an energy audit of your church building(s)? State or local government often provides such audits.

3. Are you ready to meet with your State and or Federal MP to discuss the Government / Opposition strategy to achieve zero net emissions by 2050?

4. Are there any local climate change action groups that you can link with?

Resources

A Resilient Recovery for Australia.
The Climate Council.
https://www.climatecouncil.org.au/wp-content/uploads/2020/05/report-primed-for-action.pdf

Australian Conservation Foundation. Recover, Rebuild Renew. https://www.acf.org.au/recover_rebuild_renew_lets_make_things_right_for_people_and_our_country

Decarbonisation Futures. https://www.climateworksaustralia.org/project/decarbonisation-futures/

Commission for the Human Future.
https://humanfuture.net/

Garnaut, Ross. Superpower: Australia's low carbon opportunity. Black Inc. 2019

Global Renewables Outlook: Energy Transformation 2020.
https://www.irena.org/publications/2020/Apr/Global-Renewables-Outlook-2020

Surviving and Thriving in the 21st Century. 2020. Commission for the Human Future. Canberra. https://humanfuture.net/sites/default/files/CHF_Roundtable_Report_March_2020.pdf

The Green New Deal USA https://www.congress.gov/bill/116th-congress/house-resolution/109/text

Figueres, Christiana & Rivett-Carnac Tom. The Future We Choose: Surviving the Climate Crisis. Manila Press, 2020

https://www.australianclimateroundtable.org.au/

Carbon Tracker https://carbontracker.org/

https://www.acf.org.au/stronger_cleaner_post_pandemic_australia

Future Crunch blog for the positive news https://futurecrun.ch/

www.climatechangeauthority.gov.au

Academy of Social Sciences in Australia, *Efficient, Effective and Fair Climate Policy 2020* https://socialsciences.org.au/publications/efficient-effective-and-fair-discussion-paper/

ANNEX 1
There is hope; the pace of change is surprising!

Governments, community sector organisations, corporates, international organisations, universities and research bodies around the world are working to create a renewable world. Their efforts are generating hope and producing change, the pace of which is accelerating. What is unique about the age in which we live is that their reports and statements are readily available on the internet. Here are some snippets of hope.

- Australia's major banks, insurers and superannuation funds called for a radical rethink in how to steer the economy out of the pandemic-induced economic crisis, calling for stimulus measures that are consistent with the Paris Agreement climate targets.

- *Earlier in May, Oxford University reported on a survey of more than 200 global central bankers, G20 finance ministries and academics from across 53 countries. Those surveyed were of the view that Covid recovery packages should ensure alignment to Paris Agreement commitments and set the pathway to achieving net zero emissions by 2050.*

- Mayors from many of the world's most powerful cities (including Sydney) have warned that the recovery from COVID-19 "should not be a return to 'business as usual' - because that is a world on track for 3°C or more of over-heating".[71]

- *US government's Energy Information Administration's latest inventory shows that the number of solar and wind generation sites co-located with batteries has grown from 19 paired sites in 2016 to 53 paired sites in 2019. And the EIA says this trend is expected to continue, with another 56 facilities pairing renewable energy and battery storage to come online by the end of 2023.*[72]

- A decade ago over 40% of UK's electricity came from coal. In mid May 2020, the UK clocked up its first coal free month since the advent of the power grid in 1882.[73]

- *Sweden has closed its last coal fired power station 2 years ahead of schedule, becoming the third country in Europe to exit coal.*[74]

- The World Energy Outlook 2019 Report includes a Sustainable Development Scenario that maps out a way to meet sustainable energy goals in full. It also observes that "Offshore wind has the technical potential to meet today's electricity demand many times over."[75]

- *India's achievements in the last decade in accelerating renewable capacity addition have been remarkable, according to Ajay Shankar, of The Energy and Resources Institute (TERI). Starting with less than 1 GW of solar power capacity in 2010, it now has around 34 GW of*

71 Media Release C40 Group of Mayors. https://www.c40.org/press_releases-11-mayors-unite-global-mayors-covid-19-task-force

72 Renew Economy 19 May 2020

73 Future Crunch 28 April 2020 https://futurecrun.ch/goodnews

74 Ibid

75 https://www.iea.org/reports/world-energy-outlook-2019

solar power and Prime Minister Modi has set an ambitious target of 175 GW by 2022.[76]

- Net zero emissions by 2050 or earlier is fast becoming the norm in support of the Paris climate goals to limit global temperature rise to well below 2 degrees. The list includes:

  o 121 countries, covering 25% global emissions

  o Asset owners alliance worth US$4 trillion

  o Some of Australia's largest companies

  o All 8 Australian states and territories have net zero targets in place.

- *Many recent analyses have found that Australia's electricity system can be supported by 100% renewables.*

- Within the next decade, electric vehicles are expected to become cost-competitive with, or cheaper than, conventional vehicles.

- *Jobs in renewables would reach 42 million globally by 2050, four times their current level, through the increased focus of investments on renewables.*[77]

- The NSW Government's objective is to achieve net zero emissions by 2050 by creating new jobs, cutting household costs and attracting investment. This Net Zero Plan Stage 1: 2020–2030 (Plan) sets out how the NSW Government will deliver on these objectives over the next decade.

The CSIRO says it will prioritise supporting Australia's emerging green hydrogen industry, and planning for a transition to zero net emissions, as part of a set of new research 'missions' that will guide scientific agency's response to Covid-19 and wider challenges faced by the Australian economy.
Renew Economy 12 August 2020

- *Carbon dioxide emissions from electricity generation in eastern Australia have dropped by more than 8 per cent during the coronavirus lockdown.*

- The Australian Capital Territory Government is on track to being powered by 100 per cent renewable electricity by 2020, and is committed to achieving net zero emissions by 2045.

- The New South Wales government has announced funding support for four new big battery projects in the state as it flicks the switch on the transition from coal to a grid dominated by "on demand" renewables and storage.
Renew Economy 15 August 2020

- AGL Energy has kick-started the transformation of the ageing Liddell coal-fired power station, one of biggest in NSW, lodging initial development documents for a new big battery of up to 500MW – more than three times the size of the Tesla big battery in South Australia, which remains the biggest in the world.
Renew Economy August 2020

76 https://www.cnbc.com/2020/03/03/india-has-some-huge-renewable-energy-goals-but-can-they-be-achieved.html

77 Global Renewables Outlook:Energy Transformation 2020. https://www.irena.org/publications/2020/Apr/Global-Renewables-Outlook-2020

ANNEX 2
An introduction to the evidence for Climate Change

The international scientific community accepts that increases in greenhouse gases due to human activity have been the dominant cause of observed global warming since the mid-20th century. Continued emissions of greenhouse gases will cause further warming and changes in all components of the **climate system**.[78] Four sources on climate change information are listed below, but there are many others around the world.

Intergovernmental Panel on Climate Change (IPCC)

The IPCC was created to provide policymakers with regular scientific assessments on climate change, its implications and potential future risks, as well as to put forward adaptation and mitigation options.

Through its assessments, the IPCC determines the state of knowledge on climate change. It identifies where there is agreement in the scientific community on topics related to climate change, and where further research is needed. The reports are drafted and reviewed in several stages, thus guaranteeing objectivity and transparency.

The IPCC does not conduct its own research. **IPCC reports**[79] are neutral, policy-relevant but not policy-prescriptive. The assessment reports are a key input into the international negotiations to tackle climate change. Created by the United Nations Environment Programme (UN Environment) and the World Meteorological Organization (WMO) in 1988, the IPCC has 195 Member countries. In the same year, the UN General Assembly endorsed the action by WMO and UNEP in jointly establishing the IPCC.

**To read IPCC reports visit
https://www.ipcc.ch/**

---

78 https://www.csiro.au/en/Research/OandA/Areas/Oceans-and-climate/Climate-change-information

79 https://www.ipcc.ch/

Commonwealth Scientific and Industrial Research Organisation (CSIRO)

Australia's changing climate represents a significant challenge to individuals, communities, governments, businesses, industry and the environment. Australia has already experienced increases in average temperatures over the past 60 years, with more frequent hot weather, fewer cold days, shifting rainfall patterns and rising sea levels. More of the same is expected in the future. Visit CSIRO to see the most comprehensive **climate projections for Australia.**[80]

The Climate Council

The Climate Council is Australia's leading climate change communications organisation. It provides authoritative, expert advice to the public on climate change, energy solutions and international action, based on the most up-to-date science available. A range of national and international reports can be downloaded from the **Climate Council.**[81]

Climate Change: Atmospheric Carbon Dioxide[82] **An update from NOAA.**

National Oceanic and Atmospheric Administration (NOAA), US Government.

Carbon dioxide levels today are higher than at any point in at least the **past 800,000 years.**[83]

CO$_2$ during ice ages and warm periods for the past 800,000 years

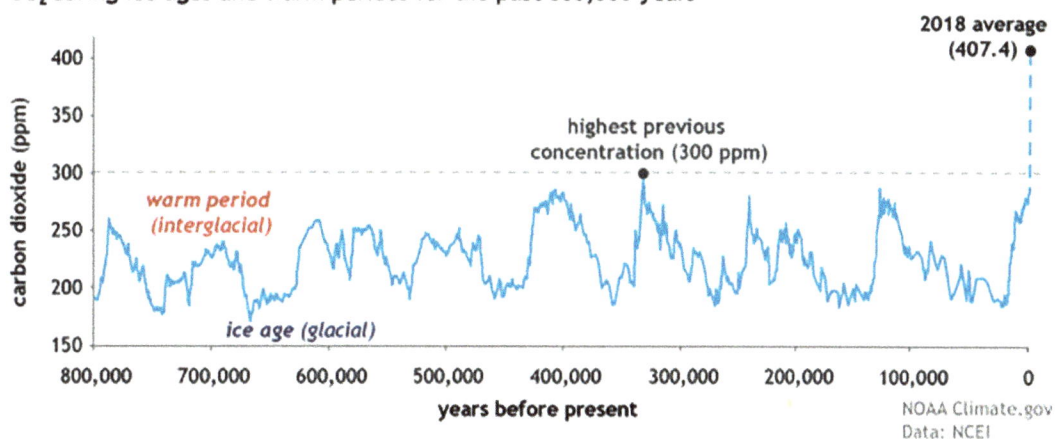

80 https://www.csiro.au/en/Research/OandA/Areas/Oceans-and-climate/
   Climate-change-information

81 https://www.climatecouncil.org.au/resource/reports/

82 https://www.climate.gov/news-features/understanding-climate/cli-
   mate-change-atmospheric-carbon-dioxide

83 https://www.climate.gov/news-features/understanding-climate/cli-
   mate-change-atmospheric-carbon-dioxide

STATES & TERRITORIES
LEADING THE CHARGE
ON RENEWABLE ENERGY

AUSTRALIA
23.5% renewable energy by 2020 (33,000GWh of large-scale renewable energy)

NT
50% renewable energy by 2030

No net zero emissions target

QLD
50% renewable energy by 2030

Net zero emissions by 2050

WA
No renewable energy target

No net zero emissions target

NSW
No renewable energy target

Net zero emissions by 2050

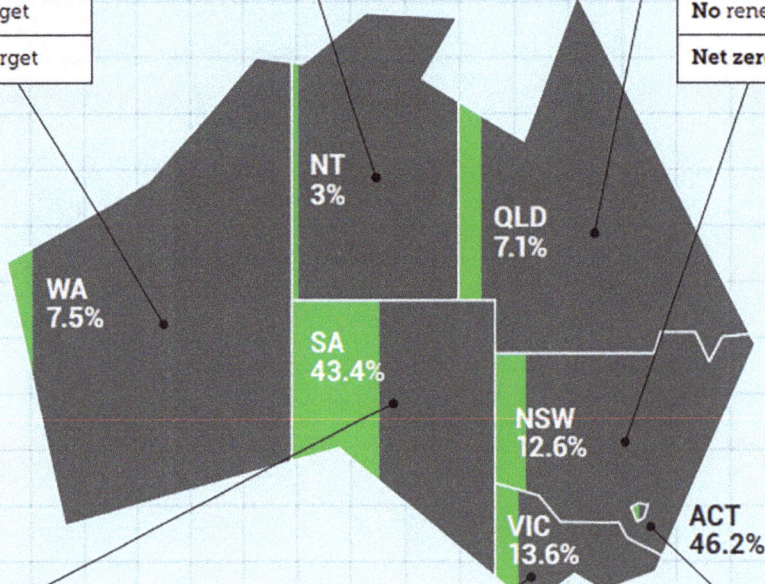

NT
3%

QLD
7.1%

WA
7.5%

SA
43.4%

NSW
12.6%

VIC
13.6%

ACT
46.2%

TAS
87.4%

SA
No renewable energy target

Net zero emissions by 2050

ACT
100% renewable energy by 2020

Net zero emissions by 2045

LEGEND
Shaded regions show the percentage of renewable energy in 2017

VIC
25% renewable energy by 2020
40% renewable energy by 2025

Net zero emissions by 2050

TAS
100% renewable energy by 2022

Achieved **net zero** emissions

Source: Climate Council

Additional ABM resources

Into the Desert

40 days of Scripture readings, reflections and prayers that take you on a spiritual journey into the Australian wilderness.

Available as an app or an 88-page booklet at

www.intothedesert.org

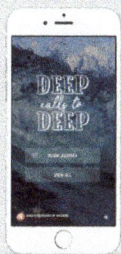

Songs from a Strange Land

Beautiful words and images to take you from Advent to Epiphany with a particular emphasis on Indigenous Christianity, the Australian landscape and Creation theology.

Available as an app or a 158-page booklet at

www.songsfromastrangeland.org

A Voice in the Wilderness: Listening to the Statement from the Heart

(with the art of the Rev Glenn Loughrey)

A study to open up conversations about the theological response to the Statement from the Heart, available as a free pdf or to purchase as a book at:

www.abmission.org/voice

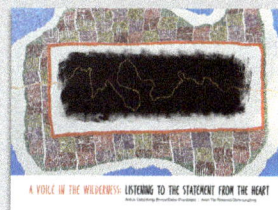

Deep calls to Deep App

(*Easter*)

A 46-day journey into the mystery of suffering that begins in Holy Week and ends on Ascension Day.

www.intothedesert.org

Where do we go from here?

Missional Bible Studies based on the book of Acts. Enter into the great adventure of 'mission' in our own time and place. In Australia. Today.

Available as an 88-page booklet at

www.abmission.org/lent

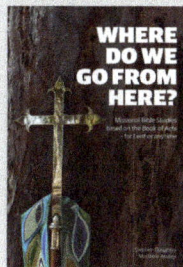

These free apps for iPhone and Android devices are available at:

www.abmission.org/apps

....

Climate for Change
Copies of this booklet can be obtained by contacting ABM or at
www.abmission.org

About us

ABM is the national mission agency of the Anglican Church of Australia working with overseas and Aboriginal and Torres Strait Islander people and communities.

We have a holistic view of God's mission. We work with Anglican Church partners and others to see lives empowered and transformed spiritually, materially and socially.

We help the Anglican Church and the wider community realise and respond to the invitation for all to be a part of God's hope for the world.

ABM believes in a world where all people enjoy God's promise of love, hope and justice. We work to see this belief become a reality.

Anglican Board of Mission - Australia Ltd ABN 18 097 944 717
Local Call: 1300 302 663
International: +61 2 9264 1021
Enquiries: info@abm.asn.au
www.abmission.org

ANGLICAN BOARD OF MISSION
Working for Love, Hope & Justice